I0083563

Divine Light

Divine Light

Michael H. Mitias

RESOURCE *Publications* • Eugene, Oregon

DIVINE LIGHT

Copyright © 2021 Michael H. Mitias. All rights reserved. Except for brief quotations in critical publications or reviews, no part of this book may be reproduced in any manner without prior written permission from the publisher. Write: Permissions, Wipf and Stock Publishers, 199 W. 8th Ave., Suite 3, Eugene, OR 97401.

Resource Publications
An Imprint of Wipf and Stock Publishers
199 W. 8th Ave., Suite 3
Eugene, OR 97401

www.wipfandstock.com

PAPERBACK ISBN: 978-1-6667-1207-0
HARDCOVER ISBN: 978-1-6667-1208-7
EBOOK ISBN: 978-1-6667-1209-4

Note to the reader

"God," "The One," and "The Friend" are used interchangeably in these poems.

Contents

Part I

On my Way to the Shrine

I

Just when the lips of The Eternal
Were about to say The Word,
Announcing the creation of a new day
From the bosom of The Night—
When the first ray of light
Began to illumine my way to the shrine,
Alone with my peaceful heart and hopeful mind—
A moan reached my ear from the singing brook,
From the source of life of my town.
Frightened to the core, I looked around.
Neither wind nor animal made a sound.
Alarmed, I stopped and looked again
With searching eyes and anxious mind:
Not a change of any kind
Except for the mournful sound of the cry.

Whether I was moved by a curious mind,
A reckless will, or a tender heart,
I cannot tell, but toward the brook
I walked in quest of the author of the moan.
At its bank I stood, and all around I looked.
All was still except the mournful sound of the cry.

Following the sorrowful sound to its source,
I walked on the sandy bank of the brook
And under an oak tree, I suddenly stood.
Again, to my left and to my right, I looked.
There, my questioning eyes spotted a flashing light
Coming from an object on the sand.
The moan took flight and with forlorn eyes
Forged a path through my ears to my heart.

Bewildered, my feet took me to that object.
I gaped at it with puzzled eyes.
"A moaning harmonica!" I wondered.
But the moaning kept streaming into my ears
Indifferent to my presence or to my bewilderment.
"How can it be? A moaning harmonica?"
I exclaimed again, more frightened than bewildered.
Alas! Should we be afraid of a mournful heart?
Oh, no! A mournful harmonica is a heart-full harmonica,
And to a mournful heart, I should speak
And with its sorrow, I should commiserate.
"You are lonely, and you are sad—
Can I ask why?" I inquired.
"I am neither a meddler nor an intruder,
I am a heart, and from the heart, I speak."

To my surprise, the harmonica spoke:
"I was made to fill the world with music;
But I cannot sing anymore: I am abandoned."
"Abandoned? I asked. By who?"
"By the hands that made me—
By the fingers that felt my cheeks lovingly,

By the life-giving air that came from his lungs,
And by the lips that blew his song through my reeds.
Without that air, how can I Breathe?
Without those fingers, how can I feel?
And without those lips, how can I sing?
My song came from the music master,
Whose song fills the world with beauty,
Whose beauty fills the mind with light,
And whose light fills the heart with joy."

"Why did he abandon you?" I wondered.
"How can a music master abandon his calling?"
"Frustration! Despair!" The sad harmonica said.
"You speak vaguely. Can you explain?"
"How can you sing without an audience,
Without appreciating, sharing ears?
· When he began to play his music
People were at first curious about his melody.
They sat here, on this sandy shore in throngs
And listened to him create magic with my reeds,
But gradually the crowds began to dwindle,
And very soon vanished entirely from his presence.
But he continued playing, hoping they would return.
Strangely, no one came back, and no one cared.

"Then his melody became sadder and sadder,
And the sadder it got, the lonelier it felt.
One evening he wept, and his tears fell on my cheeks.
They were hot, and they were sweet.
That was the last time his lips touched mine,
And his hands touched my cheeks.

He always kept me close to his bosom;
But this morning, when the first rays of the sun
Kissed this beach, I found myself alone—
Alone with myself, and alone with this stream.
The brook is desolate—listen to its murmur.
I too am desolate—by what lips can I sing?
Crushed by loneliness, I can only moan!
My moan is his song! He abandoned me
But not his mournful heart!"

Moved from a lake of sorrow, from the depth,
For that heart-full harmonica, and that mournful cry,
I asked: "Where is the music master?"
"In a cave on the side of that wooded hill."
"What does he do in that secluded place?"
"He weeps, and his weeping never stops."
"Why does he weep?" I inquired impatiently.
"Loneliness!" The harmonica said with a melancholy voice.
"His loneliness is my loneliness, and his sorrow is my sorrow."
"But why does he stay in the cave?"
"His song is his life; he cannot sing!
He cannot sing to himself, for when he sings
He is one with his song: He is his song!
Song is giving, and a singer is a giver.
He does not give pleasure: He gives himself!"

Astonished by what the harmonica said,
By the honesty of its feeling and the logic of its thinking,
I asked: "What kind of song does he sing?"
"Your question is rather strange, my friend.
There is only one kind of song in the universe!"

"One kind? What do you mean?" I asked again.
"Yes, one kind," the harmonica said confidently.
Puzzled, I stared into its trembling reeds
With the expectation of receiving and elaboration.
"The only song that is worth listening to—
The only melody the heart desires,
The only beauty the mind aspires,
And the only life the will craves is Love.
He is a passionate lover: He lives to sing.
The beauty of his song is the brilliance of his love."

"Your words are hard to comprehend, my friend!
It is prudent for me to go to the cave
Where the music master stays. The best
Remedy to the lonely heart is a caring heart.
I wish to sit by his side and share his sorrow.
But before I undertake this vital task
I should go to the shrine for my morning worship."
"To what?" The harmonica interrupted, baffled.
"The shrine!" I said, astonished to the core.
"I thought shrines have been demolished long ago
In the wake of the Great Awakening!"
"What do you mean, my friend?" I asked
"The act of love is an act of worship.
Every loving encounter is a shrine:
This holy place is the only shrine I know!"

Unaware, my eyes were lost in the reeds of the harmonica,
Without a flicker of consciousness in my mind
Or the slightest perturbation in my will--
As if I was attracted to them by some magic.

The reeds did not speak, yet they spoke;
They did not sing, yet they sang.
A breeze of peace settled in my mind,
And a cloud of warmth rained in my heart.
I saw what the human eye cannot see:
All those reeds were shining candles,
Singing and dancing in unison on The Alter,
Not in a shrine, but under The Dome,
And not in a building, but in God's open space.
Their song eddied and twirled as a spark of light,
And their light was blessing everything in sight.

They must have come from the fairest sun.
Sobs were awaiting my anxious ears
When I approached the gate of the cave.
My chest began to heave high and fast,
Without counseling my will or my mind!
I followed my legs into that dark cave!
A surge of sympathy and a waft of charity
Filled my heart to the rim, and
Bathed every one of its beats
With their sacred water, and with their holy hands.
Without knowing the path I should take,
Because the entrance to the cave was covered
With a maze of falling stalactites, still dripping water,
And a labyrinth of stalagmites on the rise.
I slithered my way through these falling and rising icicles,

But not without difficulty, and not without fear,
For the ground on which I was walking
Was covered with thorny rocks and muddy water.

And indeed, many a time I fell to my trembling knees,
But with an effort of will, I rose again and again,
Only to be covered with mud from head to toe.
But the more I fell, the more I grew
In steady direction and burning passion.
Do not ask me whence it came, or why,
But onward, I proceeded as a man of mission.
The entrance, long and meandering, was dark,
Yet in the dark, I walked and saw my way,
As if an angel was by my side and a spark was in my eye.

As I did in my encounter with the harmonica,
I followed the trail of the sorrowful sobs,
But to where I could not at first tell,
For it was as winding as the path I took
When I plowed my way through the icicles.
I was practically oblivious to what my eyes saw
Or did not see, for they were swallowed by a light,
Or to what my legs felt or did not feel,
For I experienced neither pain nor hurt.
The trail of sobs was my guide and my light.
Very soon I became one with it and it with me.
The sobs spoke a language I did not understand,
But in its wisdom, my heart understood.

The deeper I charged into the belly of the cave,
The more sorrowful the accent of the sobs became,
The more my heart roasted in the fire of sympathy.
I was aflame with a desire to touch that mournful soul,
Not with my words, and not with my hand—not at all,
But with my presence, with the warmth of my soul.

Oh, how I wanted to pierce it with the fire of my heart!
The mind melts in the fire of the heart, you know,
So does Time, for I was insensible to the flow
Of the instants, the seconds, the hours, or the days.
How can you feel this flow when it flows
From the core, when the instant becomes eternal,
And the eternal becomes an instant? I wonder!

The light in the dark that guided me
In my quest through the dwelling of the mournful soul
Grew brighter as I marched into that eternal instant,
And the brighter it got, the more arduous my trip became,
As if some spirit was toying with my will.
On more than one occasion, I had to squeeze
My body sideways between the rising and falling icicles
And forcibly pull my feet from the mud,
For it was mostly a viscous mess.
But the light that illumined my heart
Infused my will with courage, and my body with stamina.
So, I forged my way into the forest of icicles
And traversed its densest part to the end.

II

But the end was not an end: It was just the beginning!
For soon I found myself enfolded in the most brilliant light
That my eyes have ever witnessed or can ever witness.
It did not come from the sun or the moon
Or from any light made by a human hand.
At first I did not know where I was,
Whether I was standing on the ground

In a room, field, grove, or plain.
In fact, I was not here, there, or anywhere
And there was no direction or distance.
Oh, no, I was here there, and everywhere!
And yet I was more real than I had ever been
I knew I was in the presence of The Holy!

From the midst of that Light, and it had no center,
Because it was infinitely simple,
I heard a voice speak, extraordinary in its gravity!
Have you ever heard a volcano rumble
Or the earth quake before it screams under your feet?
Have you ever heard the wailing and groaning
Of Nothing crumble under the feet of Extinction,
Or the cry of Death gushing from its throat
As it splinters into nothing under the foot of God?
Have you heard the sun that melts everything,
Crackle and then shatter in the heat of its fire?
Yes, have you ever heard The Depth rumble
Or The Infinite roars in the Wilderness?
Oh, yes, have you ever heard the Absolutely Great, speak?

This Voice, which was overwhelming in its power,
Amazing in its Presence, and magnificent in its luster,
Reached my puny ears as an angry storm.
Terror permeated every cell of my body
And every fiber of my mind: I stood still—numb!
I could neither sense, feel, nor think,
And yet, in my very heart, I was a burning flame
Of sensing, feeling, and thinking-- a spark of life.
The Voice was mysterious in its tone,

Calming in its effect, and alluring in its grasp.
At that moment The Light ceased to be a flood of radiance
And it ceased to be a luminous Presence in which I stood;
It seeped into my veins and animated every drop of my blood.

I felt I was immersed in a baptismal urn
Containing the hottest water you can imagine
And kept boiling in its seething water
Until every cell of my body was purified
From all possible parasites, bruises, and infections,
And every function of my mind was purged
From all possible doubt, fear, and fantasy,
And every scintilla of my will was kindled
With the passion of courage, strength, and hope.
And yes, I felt like I was splintered into motes
And remade into a completely new being
With a new power of sensing, feeling, and thinking,
A new capacity for understanding, and a new faculty of vision.

And before I was able to regain my new consciousness,
To celebrate the new self that was emerging in my bosom,
The Voice thundered again, sending shivers to my knees:
"Why did you come to this forbidden cave?
The path you have trodden was dangerous and treacherous,
Yet you endured its danger and treachery
And proceeded in your quest without fear or hesitation.
Your aim must be dear to your heart—explain!"
My trembling knees were already escorted by quivering lips,
For I knew, and understood, the author of the voice!
A wind of fear, not the kind that comes from impending harm,
But from awe, respect, and admiration—from love,

Streamed into my heart, and into my mind.

There I stood alone, but in fact not alone,
For I was enveloped by the light of The Voice
Speechless in my mouth but speaking in my soul:
"I cannot explain, not yet, why I am here,
But I can say why I embarked on my quest."
"Proceed!" The Voice thundered again.
This morning, on my way to the shrine to pray,
My heart was attracted to a moan coming from a lonely soul.
It was tender in its tone and painful in its cry.
My heart rose to its feet and my mind to its call.
It came from a harmonica abandoned
On the sandy beach of our quiet brook.
Instead of singing, it was moaning,
And its eyes were shedding tears of loneliness!

Those tears were sparks of fire,
Intriguing in their light and alluring in their warmth.
They spoke, not to my ear, and not to my mind,
Oh, no, they spoke to the depths of my heart,
And from those depths, I sought to soothe her.
"Go to the real source of my loneliness," she sobbed.
"I am only his instrument, and I am his song.
Singing is his life. Make him sing if you can.
The air he breathes is the source of my life
And his tender lips are the source of my melody."
Feeling the fire of sympathy in my heart
And the passion in my will to seek you out,
The harmonica pointed the way to your sanctuary."

And before I made any progress in my speech,
The Voice said in a rumble: "Sympathy—you say?"
Yes, I wanted to see the melancholy face
Of that lonely soul, and I wanted to gaze
Into his eyes, hoping to enter his mind
And from there descend into his bosom,
For my arms are eager to embrace his heart,
To squeeze it until it becomes one with mine—
How else can I wipe the sweat from his brow
And the lonesome tears from his cheeks?
How else can I hear the beats of his heart?"
"And now?" The Voice thundered again,
And again it came from the depths of The Light;
But into that light I wanted to delve
In quest of the author of The Voice.
Oh, how I yearned to look upon that face—
To see the lips that had uttered the First Word
And the horizon from which all the horizons sprang.
But the "now" I now heard, and felt, was different
From the "now" I used to feel, and used to live,
For The Light that enfolded me was now in me
And the eyes that used to see things in the light
Now see from The Light and in The Light.
My eyes became one with The Light, and I one with my eyes.

An irresistible desire was rising in my heart,
A kind of propulsive power that sweeps you off your feet
Without your knowledge and without your will,
To see the face behind that thundering voice,
To stand in its luminous presence and satiate
My desire to gaze into its radiant eyes,

Touch the fingers that played the harmonica,
And kiss the lips by which he sang his song.
And yes, I wanted to embrace him with my minuscule arms
And stay close to his soul as long as possible,
For I wanted to feel the source of his moan:
How else could I feel the pain of his mournful cry?

And now, you, I want and your presence I crave!
"And you want to live from a lonely soul?"
The Voice said with sweet compassion.
"Let me confess: Your loneliness is my loneliness!
I had longed for you before I was born.
I went to your shrine and offered my prayer
As a flaming candle every morning,
Not because I needed a favor of any kind,
But because my heart was thirsty for you,
And please do not ask why I thirst for you!
I simply feel and know that you,
And you alone, I crave with all my heart!

"I want to see the radiance of your eyes,
The elegance of your face and the splendor of your smile.
"You cannot see my face!" The Voice rumbled.
"I am I, and I am not a face—neither this nor that form.
I am The Sun—neither you nor anyone can see."
"Well, the urge to condole your mournful soul
Was only a call—a call from The Depth,
Not merely for you, but for my moan-full soul.
Only such a soul can hear a moan!
Does a whole soul have room for a moan,
And does it have time to condole a lonesome soul?

Loneliness is the source of the mournful soul
Union is the only cure for this malady.

"You cannot see my face, and you cannot hear my voice.
I am faceless, and I am speechless," the Voice rumbled again.
"What you hear is the voice of The Light,
And what you see is the light of your heart.
I am The Light, and in the light, I dwell.
Without the radiance of your heart, I sink into the dark.
The moan you heard came from the bosom of The Dark.
I am The Sun, and without my light, I cannot be,
And without me, you will sink into the dark.
Your prayers at the shrine every morning
Were prayers of loneliness, of a moan-full heart;
They were prayers from you to me, and from me to you.
I wish to be in your prayers and you in mine!

"The sympathy you felt for me was a desire for union;
It was a desire to sing and dance.
Tonight you and I shall have supper under The Dome,
Then we shall go to the brook, the eternal river of Time,
And drink a glass of wine I made for you
And then sing the song you wrote for me.
Let us dance to it on the stage of our union.
The brook shall be our harmonica
And the moon and the stars shall be our audience.
Take this divine organ with you when you return
To your friends, to those who pray every morning—
Sing to them and gladden their hearts.
Let every song you sing be a ray of light.

If they cannot hear your song, dance with them
And let the light of your dance shine in their hearts,
And if they cannot see the light, cook for them,
And if they cannot eat your food, sit next to them,
And if they do not feel your presence, wait for them,
And wait there to the end of time—
Until they learn to see The Light!"

You are the Alpha and the Omega

1. Prelude

You created men and women in your image:
  They are divine.
You touched their hearts:
  They are human.
You released them from the wheel of Time:
  They are free.
You taught them how to farm:
  They are lovers.
You built the Garden for them:
  They appreciate beauty.
You planted The Apple tree for them:
  They multiply.
You showed them how to look at The Sun:
  They see the Form.
You gave them imagination
  They create.
They sat on your right side:
  They are happy.
You made them your children:
  They long for you.

2. Yearning

You are the beginning and the end,
  The Sun, the only sun, my Friend.
By its rays, I am baptized
  And by its light I see the world.

By its warmth, I feel your touch
    And by its affluence, I feel your presence.
By its grace, I feel your love
    And by its sway, I long for you.

Human love occurs as an explosion
And erupts as an earthquake, suddenly and mysteriously.
It ravishes every sensation and every passion in the mind
And sweeps up everything good and bad, green and dry, in its way
Indifferently, ruthlessly, capriciously;
And then, equally suddenly and mysteriously,
Like a mountain of snow under the blazing fire of your sun,
It melts into nothing, leaving behind a trail of devastation:
    A recalcitrant knot of guilt,
    An ironic surge of disappointment,
    And a boundless ocean of loneliness.

But my love for you is an ever-flowing river of longing,
A thrust into the depth of all depths, my Friend.
I do not seek any this or that, any now or then.
 I seek your luminous presence:
    The fire that kindles every fire,
    The cause that causes every cause,
    And the love that inspires every love!
Confess, my Friend: you long for me as much as I long for you!
Do not ask me why, and do not tease me, please.
In union, we are one, and we are we:
In union, you and I dance and sing to The One!

3. Puzzlement

But, alas! Every time I get closer to you,
You walk away from me,
And the faster I run toward you,
The faster you shy away from me,
As if you consciously try to avoid me,
As if you want to torture my tortured soul.
You baffle every fiber of my mind:
You are neither selfish nor cruel.
This I know more than I know myself.
Why this alienation, my Friend?

Your children strive for money in order to be free
    But they become slaves to it.
They fall in love in order to become complete
    But they forget that you alone make them whole.
They seek knowledge in order to understand you
    But they become dupes of arrogance.
They quest for order in an effort to find happiness
    But they trample on justice and bow to power.
They seek beauty in order to appreciate your creation
    But they worship the forms they create.
Why do you hide your face from them, my Friend?

And yet, everywhere I go, whether in the plain,
The valley, the desert, or the mountain;
Whether I think a thought, view a shape,
Or feel an emotion or examine a desire;
Whether I confront the wondrous design of the universe
Or delve deep into its infinite abyss;

Whether I contemplate the rose in my backyard
Or the grain of sand on the seashore;
Whether I mull the world of the atom
Or the largest constellation of the universe;
Yes, everywhere I go, I see your footsteps:
They point in your direction: your luminous Presence.
Why do you veil your radiance from my eyes, my Friend?

Or do you? How can the sun hide from itself?
I am baffled and in my bafflement I suffer.
Would you disentangle the tangled web of my bafflement?
You are my succor, the shelter of my life.
I sometimes think that you dwell in a crystal palace
On the top of a lonely acropolis
Contemplating the splendor of your being,
Or perhaps the wisdom of your creation,
Indifferent to the loneliness of your children—to their hell.
How can there be life without you, my Friend?

4. Whisper

My Friend does not speak--not my language, nor yours.
His Presence is his speech, and its meaning is his light.
I heard him thunder, and I heard him sigh.
I heard him laugh, and I heard him cry.
In his footsteps I walked, and before his sanctuary, I stood,
For my eyes could not stand the effusion of his light!
He must have heard the footfall of his wandering friend.
And so closer, and then closer still, I moved.
I heard him smile, and his smile was a speech.
I heard it with my heart, not with my mind,

And to my heart, it was sweeter than the honey of the gods.
Let me tell you what He whispered in my ear!

"Light I am, and veils I cannot wear.
I am I, and pure light I am.
The heart of every child is a spark of my heart:
My children are rays of my light.
They are mine, though they live in the dark.
Many a time did they fall,
And many a time did they stray from The Way.
The more they fall, the more I ache,
And the more they stray, the more I wail.
But in the end, all the roads lead to my heart."

Then he suddenly rumbled, and then He thundered:
"Without my children, I am not I,
And without me, they are not they.
Neither separation nor alienation is The Way.
Union is the beginning, and union is the end.
Beware false desire, source of all mischief:
It is the son of Nyx, goddess of the night
And perpetrator of every tumult and every plight;
A knife that spits asunder parent and child
And severs reason from the heart;
A siren that steals you away from yourself
And unawares whirls you in the heart of the dark.

"False desire is a flower of the world--
Of that which passes into non-being
The moment it comes into being,
Into the belly of that brutal Nothingness.

Think of the beauty of the rose—

 Does it not bow to the sardonic smile of autumn?

 Or the enchanting elegance of your beloved—

 Does it not lose its luster in a blink of an eye?

Or the glory of intellectual success—

 Does it not timidly surrender to the smile of vanity?

Or the sublimity of the order of nature—

 Does it not pass away with the passing of the sun?

Or the splendor of human power—

 Is it not a phantom of human imagination?

Or the titillating sweetness of the pleasant moment—

 Does it not leave a smile of sorrow after it passes?

Remember: The ultimate destiny of false desire is extinction!

"Aim high, aim at the Zenith!

Aim at The One, from which all being flows.

Aim at life, aim at The Sun.

This alone should be the ultimate object of your desire.

Bathe yourself in the light of every morning

And sleep in its lap every evening.

The Eternal is the way to The One.

Desire it, and be one with your desire.

Drink from its spring, and eat from its orchard.

Make your wine from its vineyard.

Think from its standpoint, and will from its grace.

Love from its beauty, and feel from its mind.

Gaze at its regal beauty, yes, and then smile!

The Eternal is your true desire!

"Before this desire, this flame of love,

Every other desire splinters into nothing.

Turn your eyes away from the world of show.
 Study the story of the moon, and the stars,
The tree, the river, and every object near and far.
Follow their plots to the end—the bitter end.
Aren't you tired from eating stale food,
Drinking sour wine made from sour grapes,
Socializing with people fit for a nuthouse,
And living in a stable fit for pigs?
Look into your heart, that sacred tabernacle—
Gaze into that holy spark in The Center,
And read the script of your destiny in its rays!"

He sighed again, more heavily this time.
"Their Father I am not; their Friend I am.
I long for them, and I am my longing.
I am a singer, and I am my song.
Of late, I have become a minstrel
Moving from one tavern to another,
Singing my song, my only song,
To those who drink wine from The Vineyard:
They revel in my song and dance to it.
The music of my song does not soar on the wings
Of the air that comes from my lungs
But from the fire that comes from my heart.
Alas! My song is an eternal flame of longing,
And my longing is an anxious flame of waiting."

Oh, false desire, veil of all veils,
Wall of all walls, and mist of all mists!
Oh, folly! Silence! Vanish from my attention!
I want to hold your tender hands

In a square dance with you
And I want my hands to remain locked up in yours.
Let me in your Presence dwell,
In your seething fire burn
And in your love live.
To your song, I want to listen,
And in your song, I want to melt.
You are the Alpha and the Omega!

Come Nestle by my Side, Love

Come, nestle by my side, love,
Cast your worldly cares aside,
Ease yourself into my sanctum,
Into my anxious arms,
Close to my heart.
Press your cheek to my bosom.
Listen to its beats--
Do you hear a sigh?
A yearning cry?
Let us be one in mind
And in yearning one!

A stream of tears, of warmth,
Stroked my weary bosom,
Trembling fingers clasped my arms
And a sad whisper wafted through my ear:
"One in yearning, dearest?" she asked,
"I am in your arms,
Within the grasp of your heart!
Neither space nor time sunders us!
I am baffled, speechless:
One in mind, yes,
But one in yearning—strange!"

I yearn for you the more I love you.
And love you the more I yearn for you
Now and forevermore!
"Do you speak in riddles, dear?"
Only if love itself is a riddle,

If the burning fire in my heart,
And my sighs are riddles too!
My love is boundless, firm, and constant.
My heart yearns for you
As the rose for the sun!

Let us in yearning unite, dear,
And of two minds make one!
"Love is a surge from the Depth,
A lark in flight to Heaven,
A shout from the human core
For our oneness with The One.
I am this shout!
True love is oneness of mind,
An ever-glowing sun.
Let us in one mind unite
And of two hearts make one," she said.

Do not tease me, please!
Every drop of warmth rolling on my breast
Is a languishing drop in my soul:
A drop of yearning.
I am this drop!
Yearning for you has become my destiny:
In it, I dwell, and with it, I live.
It is the light of my sun,
The dawn of my morning,
The dusk of my night,
And the present of my future!

Oneness of mind is the deathblow
To our yearning, and so of love, I said.
"Love is a union of minds," she said.
"It alone quells the pangs of yearning."
And of loving, too, my dearest,
If this is what love is,
How can I love you
If I do not yearn for you?
You, I love, and for you, I yearn.
I am fearful of a union of minds
If it quells the fury of my yearning!

"But in love, I yearn to stay,
Two hearts in one
And two lives as one.
Constant yearning is constant desiring
And so, constant hoping!
But how can I love you,
If I hope for you,
If I am caught in the wheel of hoping?
True love is constant,
And constant love is being.
I yearn to be—with you!"

No wonder Love is a goddess, dear,
A source of light, and so of passion!
Your puzzle is clear,
As clear as the light.
In love, I yearn,
In yearning I love,
And the twain is one!

"And they are one only in The One,"
She said as she pressed her flaming cheek
To my flaming cheek,
As her tears hugged my tears!

"All things—rivers, lions, and roses;
Pleasure, fame, wealth, and health;
Family, friends, and enemies—
Yes, all and knowledge too, come and go,
But, love, true love, stays,
And forever stays," she whispered.
Oh, life I seek—love in life,
And life in love I crave!
Can our love be a dance on cinder?
Wild as a tiger?
Thoughtful as a sage?

"Then, let us begin our journey to The One,
And from its infinite well,
Together, hand in hand,
Drink the water of Wisdom,
Grow, so far as lies in us,
The sense of vision, to see clearly,
The art of thinking, to know truly,
The power of will, to judge wisely.
Let us explore that fine machine—
Nature—its anatomy, its laws,
But, most of all, its Heart!

"Let us to The One ascend.
Let us to that mount, highest of all, go—

On its peak stand, hand in hand,
And with innocent eyes
Admire the beauty of The Garden,
Grasp it whole, many in one,
And blend with it, so far as we can!
Let us, in that radiant Presence,
Rest awhile, mind with mind,
Behold the Beautiful and the Sublime
And then rise with the rising Sun!

"Let us to The One go, dearest!
He is waiting for us.
Let us to that far, dark forest go,
To that quiet cloister on the eastern edge,
Where monks and nuns think and pray;
Let us in His warm lap cuddle
And from his gracious breast suckle,
Together, the milk of our life—love.
Let us become new in heart and mind,
Lead a life of adventure
In the infinite land of The One!

"Only when we drink this divine milk,
When it flows in our veins
Do we blend with The One—
Only then does our love
Fly as a lark,
Become glorious in abundance
Graceful in giving,
Lovable in loving,
And permanent in flourishing: a sun.

Only, then, yearning becomes loving
And loving yearning," she said.

Alas! The two are one, and yet not!
Does yearning grow
From the soil of loving?
Enlightenment I seek, and life I desire,
Else, my soul shall remain restless
In the dark of the night.
"My heart, where your love resides,
Is the wellspring of my light.
Love and darkness do not mix.
Satan lives in the dark.
He sold his soul to Hubris.
If love is my teacher, dear,
Then your heart is my master!

"And my heart is a tree,
Always green, always giving,
And giving because it's growing from The Depth!
Its roots are infinite, and its fruits are eternal.
The first sprouts from yearning—passion,
And the second from loving—life.
Yearning intensifies the more it grows.
It thrives not on satisfaction,
Not on fulfillment, oh, no!
But on lack of it—
On its continual urge to be whole.

"Let us to The Garden depart
And leave the treasures of this world,

Its glory, and madness, behind.
Let us on that road,
Straight, but rough, path,
Walk, arm in arm,
Heart in heart,
Two eyes in one,
And to the Garden of The One go,
Where love and yearning
Are two in one!"

When I Gaze at your Smile

When I gaze at your smile,
I gaze at a book,
The book of your life.
I do not read this book;
I see it with my mind,
Feel it with my heart,
And crave it with my will.
I become one with my gaze;
I live in my gaze!

When I gaze at your smile,
I get mad, ferociously mad.
My passion flusters:
I yearn for you.
When your eyes meet my eyes
And your lips touch my cheek
Your presence hugs my heart:
I cuddle in its lap:
It is my home

When I gaze at your smile
I feel enchanted--:
I lose my will
When your lips touch my lips,
Their flames set me on fire
Press your lips to my lips!
Press your lips harder, please!
Their heat is sweet!
Let their flames devour my heart;
I wish to be their ashes!

When I gaze at your smile,
I see a wonder:
I see a chapel—
In it, I want to pray,
In its light baptized
And by its holy oil anointed.
Kiss me, please!

When I look at your gaze
I hear a beautiful song—
Sweetest to my heart!
Its melody is wings to my soul:
On them, I want to fly,
Into your mind soar,
And into your heartland.
There I want to linger.
Gaze into my eyes, dear!

When I gaze at your smile
I see a lovely garden—
A garden of our love.
Tomorrow at dawn
Let us go to our garden
Where our red, red rose grows
And at its altar, offer our prayer.
Then let us wait a while:
We have a meeting with The One.

Yes, my dearest, tomorrow
At dawn--

When the night bows to the day
And the sun shines in the world,
And all is quiet,
Come to my sanctuary,
To my heart,
To this flame of love:
Your flame.

If Loving you is my Sin

If loving you is my sin,
Then I love to sin
And forever, I will sin!
 "But your sin is cardinal," she said.
Yes, I know! The more capital it is,
The more I desire it,
And the harsher it is,
The sweeter it is to my heart!
"Why?" she asked with a teasing look.
Because I wish to live, and forever live!

"If your sin is capital," she continued,
So is your punishment, and hell is the judgment."
Then I seek it with all my mind
And desire it with all my heart.
"But fire will consume you!
This is suicide, for you will be no more!
But I thought you loved me.
How can that be? Explain, if you please."
Alas! Into that fire, I wish to dive,
In its flames sizzle and by its blaze sputter
Until I am sanctified.
Who said the fire of hell is damnation?
Can there be salvation without sanctification?

"And how will you be sanctified?"
Let us, you and me, to that Garden go,
Among its valleys, fields, and bowers ramble,
And like bees, suck the honey from its flowers.

Let us to that Tree go and sit under its holy mantle
And with one hand and one heart pluck an apple!
"To that tree?" she said with frightened eyes.
Yes, to that very tree, I said with tender lips.
"Do you want to sin again?" she asked.
I wish to sin again and again, and forever again!
Knowing is dying, and loving is living.
I want to live and forever live!

"And how do you plan to live?" she wondered.
In my sin, and only sin, I said to her, baffled.
"But sin is bondage. Can a bondsman love?
If you cannot love, how can you live?"
On the contrary, the tree out there, our tree,
Is not the tree of knowledge, as they say.
It is the tree of love, my love for you!
Knowledge does not set you free; love does.
In love, I want to live, and in freedom, I want to be.
Every beat of my heart is a cry for you.
The key to my dungeon is not in my hand
But in your heart.
 Let me in, if you please!

"What shall you do with your freedom?
"Do you want to love me in order to be free?"
I cannot love you without your love,
I cannot be free without your freedom,
And I cannot live without your life.
The *you* in me is the we in us.
I want to live in your heart
And I want you to live in mine!

You are my foundation
And I am your destiny.
Let us to that Tree, our tree,
Go and of its apples eat—
Yes, let us sin and again sin,
Now and forever again!

I am a Fugitive

I am a fugitive!
Not the kind that runs away from justice,
Human justice, that is!
This kind of justice irritates me.
I have been indicted, tried, and condemned,
In absentia, behind closed doors,
By self-proclaimed divines.
They call themselves priests, disciples, and faithful—
God's representatives on earth,
Defenders of God and The Word,
God the Almighty, mind you,
And guardians of human happiness and destiny!
But, do I need them to secure my happiness,
To be good:
To recognize love, beauty, and truth?

II

I am a criminal,
Branded a criminal, that is!
Chased by a band of secret agents and policemen,
A militant, spiteful, ruthless lot,
Who pretend to teach the truth,
The truth of love!
Alas! And how do they teach it?
Not by love, or reason, or example, no!
They teach it by the whip, by intimidation--
By torture machines: hell and burning fire!
They manufacture these machines

In the dark caves of their souls,
Beasts in human flesh!
Really, they are bats!
Call them gangsters if you wish!

III

Do not indict me, please,
Not on hearsay, not on malicious fabrications!
Do not fear an innocent, harmless lamb!
And do not mock me!
Mock my accusers, I beg you.
I am odd, I know;
But so are you!
We are sisters,
One in two, two in one!
You understand me, then.
Look into the eyes of their patriarch!
Gaze into that supposed tunnel of truth!
Delve deep, sister!
What do you see?
An abyss of darkness--ha!

IV

I am an odd woman, a nomad,
Perhaps wayward, I confess!
And they say I am a corrupter of virtue,
Disturber of the peace,
A threat to the universal good: a renegade!

Their secret police discovered I live out of sight,
In the desert, alone! A cardinal crime, they insist!
There I ramble among the sand dunes,
Feed venomous snakes,
Dance in the sun, naked,
Eat locusts and cactus leaves,
And at night gape at the stars;
But most of all, they say,
I engage in glossolalia every dawn:
Therefore, I consort with Satan!

V

I am a fugitive, yes!
But my crime, real crime, I mean?
Well, I am in love with God,
And they know it in the depth of their hearts.
They are jealous!!
Have you ever touched God, Himself?
Have you felt His feeling?
Thought His thought?
Willed His will?
Ah! Have you crept into His lap?
Felt the warmth of His heart?
The fire of His power?
The majesty of His creative act?
The infinity of His being? Yes?
Then you are a criminal, like me.

VI

I yearn to be a fugitive—
A criminal, an outcast, a wanderer.
I yearn to be burnt, smoldered,
Yes, consumed by The Fire!
I yearn to be a flicker,
A dancing flicker
Ever dancing, upward, in this fire!
I yearn to traverse
The farthest horizon,
Farther than any limit--
To the All-encompassing!
And there before that infinite Ocean,
Stand, in awe,
Tremble, from joy,
Bow, in reverence,
And pray, in humility.

VII

I yearn to be my prayer
A glitter, a throb, a pulse of life,
In that Fire—a pulse
That can speak before the unspeakable,
Think before the unthinkable,
Desire before the undesirable,
And seek the unseekable,
That can stand, confident,
On the edge of Infinity,
On that edgeless Edge,

On that infinite threshold, yes,
And then dive into the Ocean,
Swim in it,
And drink its water—dry!
I yearn to be in it and forever remain in it.

I yearn to dive into The Ocean,
Into its depth,
Into that ultimate Source,
That eternal jewel,
Mystery of all mysteries--
Surrender myself, completely,
To its radiance,
Delight in its splendor,
Become one with it,
Vanish in it,
For a little while, just a little while,
Then return to the surface,
To my people,
Clad in a golden robe,
The robe of divine being!

IX

In this robe, I am satiated, complete—
A drop of being, of love:
I am a river of love.
Love is infinite being, you know!
Contradiction? You wonder.
I am blind to logic,
To truth and falsity

43

Good and bad,
Beauty and ugliness,
Friend and foe!
I am a source:
A spark, an ever-shining glow,
A spring, an ever-flowing stream,
A flame, ever-growing fire
Of love: the beginning and the end!

On the Sandy Shore of the Quiet Sea

On the sandy shore of the quiet sea,
Under the smiling face of the gentle moon,
On the edge of the infinite night
My love and I sat alone—
Alone with the silver rays of the moon
Listening to the song of the lonely wind
And the playful waves lapping at our feet;
Alone with the flames of our passion
And the beats of our hearts Dancing to the song of our love;
Alone with our dreams, and our secrets,
Oblivious to a past left behind
And indifferent to a future yet untold;
Alone wishing that the present moment lingers,
That it stands still forever
Under the smiling face of the gentle moon.

But suddenly our wish was swept into oblivion by the hand of Time
Taking with it all our hopes, secrets, and dreams.
My love graced my eyes with a tender smile
And embraced my face with a charming look.
To that smile, I was attracted
And in its tenderness blended.
By that look, I was captured
And to its charm, I willingly surrendered.
Oh, how liberating was that captivity
And how tantalizing was that smile!
Our eyes were locked in a silent dialogue
For an instant—an eternal instant.
Much, but not enough, was said,

And yet at that moment a flood of yearning
Surged from The deepest spring of my being
For that smile, and for that look!

With a feeling of hesitation and a dash of trepidation
I sought to recapture the thread of our dialogue,
And from the abyss of my yearning for her, I said:
"I want to lose myself in your eyes!"
Puzzled, but more amused than puzzled,
She cast a look into my yearning eyes,
One that makes your passion crackle and said:
"Do you really wish to be lost in my eyes?"
Yes, and to remain lost in them until the end of time.
"You seem to be certain of your wish, but why?"
Because I want to be reborn in the image of our love!"
"You speak in riddles, my dear. Can you explain?"
When I am away from you, I yearn for you
But when I am in the radiance of your presence
My heart is aflame with desire for you.
I wish to remain close to that spark in your heart.

"Do not mock me, please, if I say that
Your heart beats not in your bosom
And its blood flows not in its veins—
No! It beats in the vista of your eyes
And its blood flows in the river of your mind.
Within its beats, I wish to live
And in its vista, I want to ramble,
So that my eyes become one with its beauty.
I desire to drink from its river,
So that I quench my thirst for you.

I want to fly in its heaven,

So that my curious mind grows in knowledge.

And I need to breathe its pure air,

So that my heart beats as one with yours."

"Am I that important?" she teasingly asked

You are more important than importance itself!

Then staring at the dusky horizon, she said:

"You must be intoxicated this evening.

Have you forgotten that I am just a creature?"

"I have been intoxicated, and in fact, delirious.

An addict I am, and an addict I shall remain,

For I drink from the nectar of your love

Every morning so that I can see my way through the day,

And every evening so that I can see my way through my dreams.

Without this nectar, I can neither see nor breathe."

"But you should drink from the nectar of The One;

I am no more than a simple creature," she insisted.

"A creature you are not, and you will never be.

A ray of light you are, and a ray of light you will always be.

From light, you came, and in The Light, you will stay.

"There is no rank, religion or kind in The One;

The only thing I see is the effulgence of The Divine.

Light does not hide, and cannot dissemble.

What is the use of philosophy, science, or art,

Of this or that form, of this or that pleasure,

Of this or that temple in the presence of The Light?

Light I cannot see, but by it, I can see.

Truth I cannot understand, but by it, I can understand.

Every ray of light is a ray of truth

And every truth is a drop of love!
The rays of The Sun are rays of love.
Those drops are the eyes of light.
With these eyes, I can see you,
By their grace, I can gaze into your eyes,
With their help, I can soar into their sky,
And by their magic, I can yearn for you.

With trembling lips and thoughtful eyes, she said:
"If with the eyes of light you see me
And with their magic, you yearn for me,
Could it be that the light by which you gaze
Comes from the spark of your heart?
Am I what you see, or do you see you in me?
Do you love me, or do you feel your love in me?"
"No! I see you by the light of your love for me
And I love you in your love for me.
You are the fire of my will and the light of my mind.
In loving you, I love God,
And in loving God, I love you.
We are one in our hearts
We are God in our love.
Admit me into your eyes, into that holy place.
Our Friend is waiting for us there.

At the Altar of your Radiant Beauty

At the altar of your radiant beauty,
That vibrant plume of fire,
Exuberant in its brilliance,
Ruthless in its ravaging power,
Heedless in its upward thrust,
And oblivious to the ruins in its wake,
Yet alluring in its charm,
Delightful in its dance,
Dazzling in its elegance,
And mysterious in its smile—
Yes, before that brilliant beauty,
That blazing burst of life,
I want to kneel and pray!

I want to be one with my prayer,
One with that sacred flame.
Oh, how I wish to crackle within its pleats
And sizzle in its seething heat
Until every fiber of my being is reduced to ashes!
Astonished, my love asked, "To ashes?"
Yes, and, like that divine phoenix,
I wish to rise from my ashes and live again
To pray before that sacred flame again,
Only to be my prayer again and again.
"How can you make such a wish?
I feel the depth of your love for me,
But your wish eludes my understanding!"

"Beauty is the face of the soul
And the joyous smile of divine love.
It reaches your eyes, not as a kind or from
But as a blazing arrow of fire.
When your lips smile, my dear,
They dance to the radiance of your beauty,
To the flame of love in your heart.
Their dance is the dance of love—
How can I be indifferent to it?
How can I close my eyes to its charm,
My ears to its enchanting melody,
And my mind to its divine magic?
Tell me, how can I hide from that arrow?

"And that arrow does not bleed the heart.
How can it when it is a flame of love?
It is a confidant of Eros, father of The Moon.
It carries drops of honey on its feathers
And two seeds on its back—
One is a seed of want and the other of appetite:
When they grow, they become wild sparks.
One is transmuted into a burning passion
And the other into a feeling of longing.
One stings the heart and leaves sweetness behind
And the other plants a desire for more sweetness.
One leaves a desire for life
And the other incites a cry for The Eternal.

"By that arrow, I wish to bleed
And, as an invalid in medical need,
I wish to return on the back of that arrow

To the caring hands that darted it,
And before that radiant face, I wish to stand,
Not simply to look at it or adore it,
But to bathe myself in its radiance,
For I wish to go to its source, to that heart,
Where that sacred flame of fire flickers.
In that fire, I wish to burn
Until every mote of my own heart is purified.
Oh, how I desire to suck the sweetness
Of every drop of honey that drips from that wound!"

"Your words are shining gems to my eyes,
But are you certain to your mind's content
That my love is as sweet as you think it is?"
Yes, my dearest fair--of this I am certain.
It is more real than the reality of the sun
And more delightful than delight itself.
The fire that smote my heart gave life to it,
That blinded my eyes gave sight to it,
And boggled my mind gave understanding to it.
The blood that used to flow in my veins
Is now a river of life,
And the thumps that used to beat in my chest
Are now pleasing melodies to my ears!

"In your love, I delight, and in it, I shall thrive.
A skeptic I am not, but a seeker I am.
"Why do you want to be one with my heart?
Is it my beauty or perhaps your insecurity?"
In your heart and without it I shall remain homeless."
"How?" My love inquired with her eyes.

"A face can be a front, and it can be a veil,
But a beautiful face is a magical spark.
It makes you see what cannot be seen.
It has hands and can lead you by the hand.
Unlike any other hand, you have ever seen,
It can steal you from the front to the back
Of the face-- to the source of the spark.

"Behind that face, in the light of the spark,
A world of wonder spreads around.
I wish to explore its terrain inside and out:
    Drink from its water
    Breathe from its air
    Eat from its orchards,
    And play in its garden.
Yes, my love, I wish to live in your world
And cuddle in the warmth of its bosom:
    Listen to every beat of its heart,
    To every throb of its wishes,
    And to every pulse of its hopes,
And from that bosom grow, and from it live."

"What if you grow in me and me in you,
In and from our love for each other—
Is that all?" my love wondered.
"Have you heard that forlorn,
That mournful cry rising from the depths,
From the abyss, you call yourself?
It is joyful in it sadness
And magnanimous in its pain.
It comes from the mouth of Destiny, and it says:

From the spirit of love you originated
And with its gentle hands, you are fashioned.
Grow together and together rise to The Sun.
Life is a dance: Dance your way to The One.

Hearing the cry of Destiny with patient ears,
My love sent a silent gaze into my ardent eyes.
The silence of her gaze spoke loud and clear.
Moved from the depth of my mind, I said:
"Apart from you, my dear, I am not whole;
You are my eyes, and you are my light,
You are my will, and you are my passion
In our quest for The One. "But, alas!"
She said, her hand touching my yearning hand.
"How can you be whole without The One?"
Our oneness is not one without our Friend!

"The words I hear are pearls of holy wisdom, dear."
They are nourishment to my mind and to my soul.
Our love is a spark of The Sun:
From it comes and to it, it returns!
Let us, hand in hand, cultivate our tree
And give its fruits to the rich and the poor
Our love is a song to our Friend;
Let us practice the art of our song,
So you and I can, in unison, gladden
The heart of our Friend with our melody,
So that we can be one in our song with The One.

"But how can a mote be one with The One?"
My love asked with tearing eyes and trembling lips.

Bewildered, to those eyes again I surrendered.
I felt their pain and melted in their tears,
And from within that pain, I revealed a secret:
"In a sleepless night, drowned in a lake of loneliness
Crackling in the fire of Despair,
And wailing from the core of my heart—
For a breath of fresh air, and of hope—
I heard a whisper in my ear.
It came from the Abyss, I felt.
'Where have you been? I have been waiting
For you, and I have been lonely for you!'

Confounded, I sat erect in my rumpled bed,
As if I was summoned to an audience with my teacher.
I looked around for the author of the whisper.
It was not here, there, or anywhere; no,
It was in my ears, in the room, and everywhere.
I was suddenly enfolded by a luminous presence.
It sent a waft of peace into my troubled soul.
Feeling confidence in my mind, I spoke my heart:
'By doubt, I am plagued and by fear possessed.
How can I seek what cannot be sought?
How can the Infinite recognize the Finite?
I am not arrogant, not at all, my Friend.
I seek you with my mind and my soul!"

'The sun," He said, 'is luminous in its rays.
The Infinite cannot be without The Finite.
In love, I am you, and you are Me.
Love is the way, and the light, to The One.
Love is union, and in union, there is no distinction:

Neither big nor small; neither better nor worse;
Neither man nor woman; neither master nor slave.
Come to my presence, my friend, and sit in my lap.
Stay with me to the end of Eternity.
Our friends are waiting for us at the Tavern.
They have composed a song for you.
Tonight we shall drink, and we shall sing,
And we shall dance for you, my friend!'

"That night we sang and danced all in one
Until the first ray of dawn broke the night.
At first, I could neither sing nor dance.
I was out of tune many a time in my singing
And I stepped many a time on His feet in our dance,
But the hand of my Friend never left my shoulder.
He taught me how to sing, from his tender lips
And how to dance, with his caring hands.
He was with me, for me, and in me.
The fire of his heart lives in my heart.
The light of my encounter with Him
Illuminates me and invigorates my will.
Let us, heart in heart, to The Friend go!

Your beauty is a sun to my eyes,
Goodness to my heart, and power to my will.
Do not doubt this truth, if you please,
For how can the sun see itself?
But to be on the safe side, and I would,
Look into my eyes, into those shining stars!
You shall see this sun in them
In the dignity of its splendor

And the exuberance of its presence.
Every beat of my heart is a ray of this sun
And every one of these rays is a ray of life.
Let us learn how to sing and dance:
Our Friend is expecting us at his dance!

One Night, Long Ago

One night, long ago,
On the outskirts of a forgotten town,
In a tavern near The Vineyard,
I drank a glass of sweet wine.
It was delicious to my taste and to my heart.
I drank and sang with your merry friends all night long.
The more I sang, and the more I drank, the merrier I got.
I drank more of your sweet wine, yes, I confess!
I have been intoxicated ever since
Swirling in a sea of yearning for the Wine-maker,
For you, Maker of the sweetest wine!

In The Vineyard, I went looking for you
With anxious eyes and a heavy heart.
Oh, how I crave your company!
I want to gaze into your dreamy eyes,
Into that infinite ocean of your Presence,
And ramble in the garden of your heart.
I want to sit next to the Fountain,
That ultimate source of life, and of light,
Drink a cup of its holy water,
And become a fountain in your Vineyard.

"A fountain?" I heard a whisper from the Depth.
"Yes! My heart longs for The Fountain.
I crave your luminous Presence:
I want to sit in your lap, within your arms,
Listen to the beats of your heart
And the song of every beat.

I want to be there at the crack of dawn,
Everlasting Dawn,
When you illuminate the world with your light
And water every one of your vines.

I don't want to be intoxicated, not anymore.
I want to be a source of intoxication: a wine-maker,
Not one who shops for merriment at the tavern,
But one who makes merriment possible,
One who gives, and in giving, receives.
And I seek the intoxication of giving, not receiving.
How else can I hear the song of your heart?
Doesn't the world flow from its melody?
How else can I dance to the beats of your heart?
Doesn't' the world receive its pulse from those beats?
Yes, I desire to dance with you, my Friend!

Let us Be Two in our Adultery,
and One in The One

"Lately you have been acting strangely, dear!
You are so distracted, you hardly acknowledge my presence.
Your lips used to greet my lips every morning,
But now you kiss me on the cheek.
Your right hand used to caress my body in bed every night,
But now you hug me as if I am your sister.
You used to enjoy the meals I cooked for you,
But now you hardly finish the meals I cook.
You used to share your feelings and dreams with me every day,
But now you seem to live in a different world.
What is wrong, my dear? Why have you closed your heart to me?
I am the same woman who loved you and will always do.
Your worry is my worry, and your happiness is my happiness.
Reveal the cause of your distraction to me, my love."

"What you say is true, truer than truth itself," I replied.
"Your loving is greater than love itself,
And your heart is purer than purity itself.
From you, I cannot withhold my feelings or dreams,
And I never have, so far as I know.
But my neck is clasped by a hand greater than the hand of Death—"
Stunned, my love cried: "Greater than the hand of Death?
Please, tell me about this cursed hand.
Death kneels like a lamb before the eyes of love."
Somewhat hesitant, I said: "Guilt—the cardinal kind!"
"What do you mean? What crime have you committed?"
She asked with a deep feeling of fright.
"I have betrayed you. I am an adulterer."

A river of tears flowed over my love's cheeks.
Then she looked at me with wailing eyes and asked:
"Why? Have I denied you anything? Who is she?" She asked.
You have not denied me anything, and I doubt it is a she."
"Then my calamity is greater than I thought," she said.
And from her wailing eyes, my love asked again:
"Who is he? Is it a she? You speak vaguely, dear."
"Well," I began, "as I was strolling in the moonlight one night
Dreaming a sweet dream about you, about us, a few days ago,
Something extraordinary happened to me: The one, yes, He,
Appeared to me in the face of The Moon, our friend.
He was not merely beautiful, but the living radiance of The Beautiful.
His smile was not merely charming, but the living warmth of Charm.
He was so elegant, so enchanting, so overwhelming,
I could not help but fall in love with Him.
Now His radiance fills my heart:
There is no room in it for anyone or anything.
I consciously and willingly surrendered myself to His arms.
I am guilty, I know, but, if possible,
Would you accept me as an adulterer?
I have been having meetings with Him every night."

The river of tears flowing over my love's cheeks
Was suddenly transformed into a river of joy.
Without saying a word or making a gesture of any kind
She rose to her feet, embraced me warmly,
And then coyly replied: "Yes, I do!"
"You do?" I asked, fearing that she would never accept me again.
Yes, she assured me again.
Then, gracing me with a lovely smile, she added,
"I have committed the same crime, my dearest!"

And you too? I exclaimed, delighted.

"Are you unhappy, my dearest" She asked.

No, I am happier than the angels in heaven!

Then, with two happy eyes, she added:

"Let us, my love, be two in our adultery and one in The One!"

Before the Maple Tree

As though seized by an alien force,
I suddenly stopped before that old maple tree,
That proud, green burst of life,
That unyielding thrust into the higher depth--
The same tree that greeted me cheerfully
Every morning when I went to work
And every evening when I returned to my home—
Yes, clad in her autumn gown, before the maple tree I stood,
But today I did not stand before the same cheerful complexion,
Not the same vibrant dance of life—no!
I stood before a heavenly sight: a divine dance.

Before the golden wires of the setting sun
The brazen leaves of my friend were falling carefree,
As if they were dancing to the golden sun,
As if they were celebrating the sacred rite of life,
Indifferent to the pull of gravity, Pied Piper of existence!
Caught unaware between the elegance of the dance
And the seductive charm of the Pied Piper's music,
Between the upward thrust of the tree
And the downward slide of the falling leaves
My heart trembled, and my lips quivered.
A lonely tear rolled down my cheek.

There I stood transfigured within my tear, baffled.
But my bafflement deepened in depth and breadth
When one of the cheery leaves stopped
On edge— indeed in mid-air among the falling leaves—
As if she did not want to disturb the divine dance,

As if she wanted to reveal the radiance of her beauty,
Or perhaps to invite me to the divine dance.
I looked at that scene with unbelieving eyes,
With eyes that were seeing what no eyes can see.
As fear toyed with my timid soul,
I cried: "How can it be? It cannot be!"

"How can it be?" A voice came from the tree.
"Questions of what can and cannot be are irrelevant.
What actually is, is entirely different from what can and cannot be
And transcends both in dignity and splendor.
In The Sun all diversity melt into one
And the one into the infinite being of Truth."
Frightened out of my wits, in the core of my being,
I searched everywhere for the author of these words,
But neither human nor animal was around.

Alas! I cried. Am I losing my mind?
"Not at all!" The voice spoke again, this time, tenderly.
More confounded than puzzled, I looked again, everywhere,
But everywhere was nowhere, for all was silence.
But, like a bolt from the blue, my search was arrested
By a curious glow emanating from that leaf—
And from that very leaf, the voice spoke again:
"Look not with your eyes, but with your heart;
Your heart is your eyes, your ears, and your mind.
The truth, and everything real is light, pure light;
It is not image, or thought, or form of any kind!

"A leaf stops in mid-air? A leaf speaks?
A leaf-- a glow of light? Am I hallucinating?

Am I in the age of miracles?" I wondered.
But I was wrong, for the voice returned again:
"Does it matter where the truth comes from—
Whether from a child or a sage, a tree, or a bird?
Or does it need the approval or the signature,
Of the philosopher or the scientist,
The artist or the theologian?
Free yourself from these idols, from these despots!
Listen not to me, to this lowly leaf!
Listen to your heart, to that shining spark!

"Always remember: The language of The One is eternal silence,
Not the silence of nature, of this woman or that man,
But of the kind that speaks the language of the light,
That speaks the unspeakable without speaking!
Do you speak with your beloved or even whisper,
When your eyes lose themselves in hers?
When you sizzle with joy in her bosom?
When every fiber of your mind, and your body,
Crackles from the fire of your love?
When you want to consume yourself in that fire,
Or when you will that fire to kindle eternally?"

I tried to speak, but my lips quivered,
And my eyelids lowered—yes, from perplexity:
I understood what my ears heard, but I did not understand.
The truth weighed heavy on my weary mind, so I asked:
"How can you dance the dance of life,
And how can you swirl gracefully to the smile of Perishing
When you know you are easy prey to its charm,
When you know that you are on your way to extinction?

The golden rug under the mantle of the tree
May seem a bridal bed, but it is a bed of death.
Into that silken bed, you are falling!
How can I but wonder, if not rebel, against your fate?

"But that bed spreads around you, too, wherever you turn,
In the valley, the mountain, the river, and the plain!
Could it be that the air you breathe is the air of extinction?
The same sun to which you are dancing is a fire,
I confess, but it is the fire of death.
What baffles my mind is not merely a logical contradiction,
But the contradiction of being, of how can
That which is good and beautiful, and even the true,
Sleep in the bed of death—forever!
Before this spectacle, I stand, but do I stand?
Is the scene I am now seeing a show in my mind?

"I am as real as the dance you see," she said,
"And as real as the scene you wonder about.
What is real cannot be and not be.
If it is, then it is, and forever it is.
If it passes into extinction, then it never was.
Specious logic I do not think and I cannot.
The logic of being I can speak, and I do.
I am brazen, I know, and in that bed, I shall sleep;
But I am I, as real as the sun!
Who said I cannot wear a different gown
Or sing a different song to The One every dawn?"

"You can sing, and you can dance, the way you choose,
And you can perform miracles if you please,

65

But I am certain your autumn gown will soon fade
And will cease to exist before my eyes and yours.
I have been watching your sister leaves
Every season and every day fall to that cursed bed.
For them, my heart was wrung with painful tears.
If logic you speak, speak the logic of pain.
Don't mock me, please, not my good sense!
Don't you negate what you say by your own words
And by the very act of falling into that bed of leaves?

"Into that bed, I shall fall sooner than you think
"And with my sister leaves, I shall weave
A tapestry of beauty for your eyes to please
Every morning when creation wakes up
And every evening when it goes to sleep.
Think not from the standpoint of the human race
And feel not from the vantage point of the human heart
But from the perspective of this leaf and every leaf.
Leave the dark cave in which you now live.
See with the innocence of the child
And feel with the passion of the philosopher.

"Free your mind form the wheel of time
And your heart from the concerns of the world.
Look upward! Look into the sky of The One,
Into the infinite ocean of freedom.
Learn to be a lark—to fly into the Depth.
When you arrive, go to the mountain of Abundance.
Ascend it slowly, and then sit on its peak and look around.
Examine how the wheel of time, that enigma of creation,
Spins the seasons, the days, and the years,

And learn how it weaves the infinite world of space,
Of stars and planets-- of this, that, and every place.

"On the ledge of that peak, sit and wait
Until The Sun rises, and it will rise only for your eyes,
Therefore, will it with all your soul and all your might.
Then, and only then, will you learn how to see.
You cannot clearly see unless your vision
Is baptized by the golden rays of The Sun.
Then your eyes will see the light, and in The Light.
You are not a mind without this light
And you are not a heart without this spark.
Can your friends recognize you, or you, yourself,
And can you love them, or love yourself, in the dark?

"From life, I am, and to life, I am destined.
My life is a dance, and in every motion I go through,
Be it a petal, a leaf, or a shade-maker,
Wherever or however you see me, I am a dancer,
The same dancer who sings, weaves, and gives life,
And I am more: I am an artist; I am a surge of life!
Can the sun shine without its light?
Can the light exist without its sun?
The sun is not the light, true, but the two are one.
Think with your heart, not with your mind, my friend."

To my surprise, the words the voice spoke
Were not drops of sound, for I did not hear them.
First, they coursed through my veins as stakes of fire
And then they streamed into my heart as rays of light,
For I saw them, and what I saw was radiance before my mind.

With trembling legs and fingers nestling in my hands
I wondered: How can words be drops of light?
"They can," my friend, the dancing leaf, replied.
"If you can think what you see,
You can see what you think,
And what you see is light, and nothing but light."

But my surprise became a storm of puzzlement
When I looked at the leaf again.
Lo and behold! The dancing leaf was no more!
It stood between the falling leaves as a boundless glow.
I could not tell whether this radiance
Came from the leaf or perhaps from my eyes,
For I was enfolded by the warmth of its splendor.
Have you ever seen a smiling glow or a glow in a smile?
"Do not speak in riddles!" I hear you say.
Well, if what you see is a riddle, in riddles do I speak.
But goodness! What is a smile but a glow of life?

Part II: Divine Light

Divine Light

Part I

I am an eccentric man, a prowler, if you like,
Who lives on the fringe of civilization,
And wanders in the streets of the night--
The agitated night of the human soul.
Call me an insolent snoop if you choose.
I have heard some decent people
On whom I furtively spied,
Use more interesting epithets.
Name-calling does not mean much.
The ancient gods are my forebears;
They too were prowlers of the soul.
Prowling is an art of surprise—
Of catching you in the act.

I thrive on agitation—Chaos.
Chaos is alluring, seductive.
Even the Almighty, yes, The Perfect,
Was seduced by the agitation of Chaos.
How else am I able to write these words,
Fight for freedom and justice?
How else can the corn grow in the field,
The wind blows from the north,
Or the stars glitter every night?

Alas! A prowler is a compulsive thief,
A thief of the most valuable treasures—
Not of the body, and not of the world:
These treasures are repulsive to my taste!

I am enamored by the human soul.
It is here, there, but nowhere!
It haunts me everywhere I turn—
In the factory, the farm, and the garden;
In the library, the hut, and the lecture room;
In the temple, the plain, and the battlefield;
In the monastery, the prison, and the music hall;
In the hospital, the nursery, and the torture chamber.
I seek the mind of the human soul:
To see its eyes—where they look,
To feel its passions—why they cry,
To touch its heart—why it throbs;
To know its will—what it wants!

Do not think I am an arrogant man.
I despise arrogant people and their friends.
They are intellectual midgets—flunkies.
The mere sight of them irritates me
And I shun them like the plague.
But sometimes I cannot avoid them,
Especially when I visit taverns.
Here, in these questionable places
You meet people you love and admire,
And people you detest and avoid.
The detestable people and they are many,
Come here to affirm their perceived significance.

The lovable few come to get drunk.
I spy on lovers and the lovable.

And yes, I seek lovers in taverns,
Not in churches and universities,
But in some neglected corners—
In the dark, away from the noisy crowd.
These types of people are lovers of silence,
Not the silence of the fool
Nor the silence of death,
Oh, no, not the silence of absence,
But the silence of presence: life.
Here, in this kind of strange silence,
In a tavern on the edge of my town
I saw him gazing into the dark!

He was oblivious to the clamor around him,
To the merriment of his fellow drinkers—
An island of tranquility in a sea of noise.
Who could resist such a drinker
Or the opportunity to drink his way?
"Can I join you?" I ventured,
Disturbing the serenity of his gaze.
He did not speak, but, instead,
A most irresistible, welcoming smile
Radiated from his ruddy lips.
Unaware that I was already seated
Within the range of his gaze,
I felt a nagging urge to speak.

Confused, and with quivering lips,
I timidly asked, "Are you He?"
Surprise itself pierced through his eyes,
But trepidation gripped my heart:
"He? Who?" He humbly mumbled.
A glow of peace illumined his face
And doubt swept through my anxious mind.
"Am I foolish? Am I sane?" I wondered.
Then I gaped at his face again.
A dazzling ray of light shone from his eyes.
An insistent feeling of confidence, and of joy,
Danced its way to my consciousness:
"It is He, yes, the awaited One!"

How can the human tongue speak
In the presence of divine radiance?
And yet, my dear, my frightened tongue
Spoke by the grace of divine radiance.
It spoke in the light of the Dark,
In the darkness of the light around!
"The Son of God!" I finally said.
A halo of amazement crowned his face.
A breeze of compassion blew from his eyes
And a gentle smile flowed from his lips:
"A glass of red wine?" He intercepted.
"I would very much enjoy one with you!"
Still gazing at me, he filled my glass.

"Red wine?" I recklessly asked.
It was a slip, some would say.
"Of course, try it, if you please!"

The wine I drank was nectar, dear—
Not an ordinary kind of wine.
An extraordinary waft of warmth,
Indescribable, enchanting warmth,
Spread throughout my heart.
Then I focused my eyes on his.
His gaze had already settled on my face.
Alas! He understood my innermost desire.
Secrets of the heart cannot be spoken
But must be understood in the silence of the soul!

"Are you He?" I tried again.
He gently lifted his glass of wine
And before he took a sip said:
"To your good health, friend!"
His words were hugs, my dear.
They were familiar music to my ears.
"I am not the man you think I am.
After I was crucified and buried
My friends became mythmakers.
They reveled in hero-worship,
Not in The Light, not in The Truth!
They were butchers of The Truth!
I was not the man they said I was."

"Then, who are you?" I cried.
"And yet, you are He, and no one else!"
Sparks of curiosity flew from my puzzled eyes.
They did not fade into ashes, forlorn,
And they did not fall on desolate ground
But landed on the shore of his cheeks,

On his comprehending, compassionate eyes.
Smiling to my eager, artless lips,
To my searching, tortured soul,
He gently poured more nectar, more life,
Into my thirsty glass.
A lonely thought crossed my weary mind:
"Is he playing the game of the gods?"

"I am not the Son of God, nor God;
On the contrary, God is the son of man."
Fire streamed from his wild gaze.
Then, as if returning from an ineffable vision,
And thrusting his look into my frightened face,
He exploded, "Man created God!"
Wetting his throat with a sip of wine, he added:
"Man created God in his own image;
He created a mega-man, yes, he did,
From the ashes of his own corpse!
In this criminal act, this crime of crimes,
Man forgot all about The One, his source,
And so, all about man himself!"

"Crime of all crimes!" I echoed impulsively.
With a twinkle of sarcasm on his lips
And a spark of fire in his eyes, he continued:
"Instead of one, man committed two crimes,
One against himself, and the other against The One."
The blazing fire in his fugitive eyes
Streamed, like lightening, into my mind.
"What do you mean, friend?" I interjected.
"Fabrication! Your God is a fictitious god!

Your holy God is a lie to the people
And to The One, the really true One,
Fashioned in the mind of Hubris itself.

"Your holy God stands as a dark abyss,
As a polluted sea, yes, as a hostile barrier
Between man and The One, man and himself!
It has become a grave, a rotten grave—
A tomb, they call Church, was built on it.
Its epitaph reads: 'Here lies The Truth!'"
Suddenly he stopped, took a breath,
And with trembling lips resumed his invective:
"Light! Think with me—light is life!
Where can you go without light, ha?
Can anything, including eternity, be without light?
Darkness is the source of forgetfulness
And forgetfulness is the death of man, and God!"

"Your words, friend, fell upon my mind
As drops of revelation, of enlightenment,
And into my heart as drops of honey.
They are bright stars in the night of my soul,
For which my heart shouts with gratitude.
This precious gift, this ray of bright light,
Inclines my curiosity to ask again:
Who are you? Why are you here—
Here in this tavern among the lost?"
The fire in his eyes was replaced by compassion.
A gentle smile floated over his tender lips.
A dialogue thrived between his eyes and lips.
His lips spoke from the depth of his eyes.
I believe his soul dwelled in his eyes.

Casting a thoughtful yet painful,
Look into my face, he murmured:
I am a human being, and I am a renegade.
My fellow prisoners said I worshipped The Light.
This piece of gossip reached the ears of the guards.
I was exposed to the world as an apostate—
A corrupter of the youth and a disturber of the peace
And then to the Supreme Court as a heathen:
A threat to the common good and the faith.
Light, my dear, can blind the eyes, and the heart!
In his wisdom, the master, their primate,
Reasoned that I had lost the way, their way,
And that I was in urgent need of reform.
"Having deliberated in the utmost of their wisdom,
The Council placed me in the master's custody."
After a patient stare at his wine glass,
He said: "He took me to his castle—in the desert."
The eagerness, which oozed from my face
Succumbed to an expression of suspense.
My blood suddenly halted in my veins.
I became a volley of heartbeats!
"A castle in the desert! The irony of ironies!"
"Yes, it is an irony, a travesty of reason.
You must be ready for another glass of wine!"
He filled my glass, and he filled his too.
Then he embraced me, gently, very gently,
With his luminous eyes, with his light.

His light was the light of peace.
"Were you reformed? How?" I pleaded.
The primate had compiled a vast file about me—

Where I lived, what I said, and what I did.
He understood me, and I understood him.
Thirty moons passed over the castle.
Silence ruled my lips with an iron will.
But my eyes spoke my mind loud and clear.
Alas! The patience of men is sharp and short.
On the tenth moon, he broke his silence:
"I would give you the grandest castle in the kingdom,
With all the pleasures your heart desires
If you desist from your quest for The One!"

My ears heard the temptation,
But my eyes spoke, and in silence, they spoke.
He understood my silence, and he expected it.
Sparks of fury flew from his face,
From the depth of spite itself, in my direction.
I was carried on this fury back to my dungeon.
Then on the twentieth passage of the silver moon,
Who became my solace during the night,
I was presented, again, to his Excellency, the primate.
There I stood alone, hands in shackles.
Quizzically his look devoured my eyes,
Hoping to see a change in my heart,
For my heart dwells in my eyes!

But my heart was as sound as the soundness of the Sun.
"'I shall install you as the king of the land
If you desist from your pursuit of The One."
Neither my mind nor my heart was perturbed.
His piercing eyes saw the truth of my mind.
Silence was the only language I spoke,

And he was a master speaker in this art.
Gloom slowly spread on his frigid face.
Instantly flashes of malice flew from his angry eyes.
They fell defeated around my naked feet.
But anger grew in his eyes by leaps and bounds.
With a slight motion of his fiendish finger,
Hands in shackles, I was taken to my vault.

"The gentle moon, my only friend, smiled at me every night.
She was a monument of hope, of silver light.
Almost famished from hunger for thirty days,
I was summoned, again, to the royal throne.
His face was as grave as the grave of the dead
And his vengeful eyes as the vengeance of Satan.
Their vibes fled in my direction, and he declaimed:
'This is the end of the road—the end of your life.
You are a menace, a disturber of the peace.
Our people do not need love, and they do not need light.
They are happy in the cave of man—their home.
They detest your freedom and your kind of joy.
Love burdens their hearts, and light blinds their eyes.

'You shall be tortured, and you shall die on the cross
If you do not desist from your pursuit of The One.
This is the judgment of the Court, and this is the end.'
Sharp, deep furrows loomed on his forehead.
Twittering drops of sweat rolled between them
And his eyes sparkled with anxious expectation.
Our eyes were clasped in a prolonged conversation.
But calm ruled my soul, and silence ruled his lips.
Drowned in frustration, he looked at me in consternation.

Tears quivered in the corners of his eyes
And love blazed in the depth of my heart.
We parted, but not the conversation of our eyes—
He to the chamber of his glory, and I to my dungeon.

At dawn, when the birds were singing and dancing,
I heard the hammers pounding—for my cross.
'Your end is near!' A voice whispered in my ear.
'And then added: 'Life is good, and life is dear!
Choose and be clear: life or death?'
An overwhelming consciousness from the depth
cried loud and clear: Choose life, not death.'
But I mused to myself: 'what is life?
What is life without light, and light without The One?'
My musing resonated in the desolate halls of my mind.
It was interrupted by more pounding and less musing.
'Your end is near!' The voice whispered again.
A soft ray of light slithered into my dungeon.

"The end has arrived? But, alas! Has it?
What is an end, a beginning, or in between?
How did these landmarks come into existence?
Where do I fit in these silly fictions?
My mind was still preoccupied
With these fetters, these fictitious fetters,
That enslaved the minds of people everywhere,
When I heard a commotion of whispers at my door.
I was standing in the light, in that holy ray,
When a group of men clad in arms
Knocked, entered, and then with their eyes
Spoke: "Are you ready?" This signaled the end!
They looked fierce and mighty, but they were sheep.

"In shackles—shackles still?" I pondered.
"Are they afraid? Of what? Of light? Of love?"
Suddenly the locks, and the shackles,
Were removed from my fragile, helpless hands.
Then three armed men carried my pliant body,
Two holding my hands and one holding my legs,
Placed it on the cross, stretched it on the ground,
 Firmly fastened my hands and my legs to the boards.
'Are you ready?' Roared a voice from nowhere.
'To me, or to my executioners?' I reflected.
'I am ready. Let it be!' I continued.
The armed men stood erect with hammers and nails
Cast a final look at my peaceful eyes!

My vision was lost in the infinity of the blue sky,
In the depth of its sublime beauty,
When, abruptly, the four pillars of my being,
Trembled and shuddered, shuddered and trembled,
When a torrent of pain, unbearable and indescribable,
Gripped every organ and every cell of my body.
Involuntarily a wild, ear-splitting shriek,
Rising from the core of my frightened soul,
Stopped in my throat, hesitated a little,
Then exploded against its solid walls: dead.
The nails were in, and I was one with the cross.
Never did my mind know such devastation;
Never did it experience the guile of men: hell.

And from this very hell, my consciousness recovered,
But not from its fire, not from its brutal claws.
My pain was quickly growing into agony

And my courage was feeling the test of its endurance.
My cross was no longer lying on the ground
But standing vertically on a low pedestal.
The moment my eyes opened to the world,
Having paid a short visit to the unknown,
They met a pair of grave, motionless eyes,
At a window across the square from my cross,
Watching the eloquent scene of my hell
And seeking a conversation with my tearing eyes.
I understood the meaning of the inscrutable look,
And I understood the purpose of the hell he devised.

Blood was dripping from my punctured hands and legs.
The holes were centers of radiating fire,
The fire the primate had designed especially for me.
My heart was silently crying and wailing.
Shocked by the scene of its living hell,
I still made an effort to keep my two eyes open
To have a conversation with those two enigmatic eyes.
'What does he want from me after all this?
More cruel means of torture?' I thought.
'How hard can the human heart be?'
Some mysterious power energized my vision.
I was able to steadily hold his gaze,
Its oppressive intent, its unyielding determination.

My gaze stood its ground: we spoke one more time.
He gave an approving nod, a slow, arrogant nod,
 A forceful repetition of the earlier temptations:
"You still have time—you can recant, yes,
And you can regain your freedom and your glory

If you desist from your quest for The One."
My spinning head collapsed against my chest.
And a cloud of pain rained more drops of agony into my soul.
The wheels of my hell were grinding faster and faster.
With an effort, I did not know its source or how,
I raised my head and with it, my eyes, in his direction.
A waft of love flew from my heart to his eyes,
It must have died on the fringe of his barren heart.

His eyebrows widened and, his chin quivered.
A beam of anger dashed from his angry eyes
And landed on my peaceful face, at my loving gaze.
Neither peace nor love did he want, or prize;
Meekness and submission he demanded.
The agony that flickered around my battered face
Was crowned with a shimmer of compassion.
His angry gaze was fractured by its scent.
Compassion was repulsive to his ego, to his pride.
Suddenly his complexion, furious and vengeful,
Reverted to its solemnity: deadly composure.
He looked at my dangling head one more time
And nodded to the armed men around me.

A bustle of whispers, frightened and confused,
Shattered the chilly silence of the square.
I felt three cayenne-saturated sponges nursing my wounds
Only to be followed by an eruption of pain in my body:
A volcano spitting one lava of agony after the other
Choked every pulse of life in my veins.
My belly convulsed, and my chest responded.
A flood of nausea gushed through my nostrils.

My tremulous lips murmured: 'Why? What for?
Sickness unto death—is it? Is there an end to this?'
The hell men create seems stronger, more violent,
Than the body can bear and the mind can imagine.
In moments of weakness, cursed doubt rushes in!

In the hell of men, time does not exist.
You do not count days, months, or years.
Their hell is an eternal stretch of agony.
You know the meaning of agony, what it is like,
Only when you live the meaning of true life.
A glimmer of consciousness crept slowly, ever so slowly,
Out of this stretch, out of this numbness,
In which I must have been drowned for some time.
The volcano of pain was still spitting balls of agony
And the dark cloud of nausea was still raining
Arrows of deathly revulsion into my soul
When a spear of fire pierced my right side.
'More torture? This must be the end! Why?'

The bustle of whispers passed into deadly silence.
The throbs of my agony crashed on its walls—
On the walls of my consciousness, as if to say:
'This is the end! Have you chosen wisely?'
Well, the new wave of blazing fire, perhaps the last,
Resounding in every cell of my frail body,
Intercepted this short rumination with a shock:
A frenzied surge of awareness grasped my mind,
Not because my body was up to it—no,
But because of the intensity of my agony.
Impulsively my eyes opened up one more time

To the world, to its light, light of the royal castle,
Light of the kingdom of the people, of their wisdom and destiny.

The same pair of eyes, and the same chilling gaze
That examined me, judged me, and decided my fate,
Were waiting for my eyes, and in the same window.
Once more, the space between our eyes collapsed.
It was another intimate moment—final, irrevocable.
It was a flame in the fire of my hell—his own creation.
'Is he trying to crush me—pulverize my will,
Then ask me to converse with him, on his terms?
Where is the heart of people—the justice of people?
From my eyes, from the burning flame I had become,
Came a faint whisper: 'I want to live! Why not?
I am a man, after all, like the rest of them!'
A sinister frown flaunted on his furrowed forehead.

His lips were tightly sealed, but not his eyes,
For they lashed at me with a loud shout:
'I know you want to live! Yes, I know!'
And with a sarcastic smirk, he continued:
'You can still live, if you choose life—our way,
If you desist from your pursuit of The One.'
'But I seek the true life: the life of The One.'
My silent words were wrinkled by my own flames,
So was every organ of my wasting body—slowly.
Their onslaught was moving in every direction.
In the midst of that waste, that wretchedness,
My consciousness was clutched by the neck
With two steely hands, the hands of fear, saying:
'Desist! Choose life, their way, or death!'

'Remember, you are only a man,' the voice added,
'Your cross is the end of the road, of your life.'
'Yes, I am a man, only a man,' I reflected,
'But I crave the light, light of The One—why?'
Then a spasm in my heart ravaged my mind.
My eyes quivered, and my consciousness flickered.
His gaze became blurred but remained in place
Waiting for an answer from my weary eyes.
My vision was obstructed by a multitude of images
Accompanied by clusters of emotions and ideas.
Rays of light were dancing between, and around, them.
I did not understand the meaning of the images and the ideas,
But I understood the meaning of the rays—their delicious dance.

And with it a faint smile danced on my lips.
As if waking from a reverie, I tried, once more,
To meet the gaze of my prosecutor: the primate.
But he had vanished into the darkness of his castle.
My decision was made, and my destiny was determined.
I returned to the crackling flames of my hell.
The whispers of the armed men grew fainter and fainter.
My dangling head was getting hotter and lighter,
But, most of all, my consciousness was fading.
Yes, it was a strange, and I am certain, a baffling fact:
The brutal and debilitating assault of my hell dwindled,
The agony of my turbulent soul subsided,
And the anguish of my mind died—in silence."

 My eyes were drowned in a pond of tears
When the stranger fell into solemn silence
With the silence of his anguished mind.

My tears were hidden from his sight;
By the dimness of our booth—our solitude.
His silence, though, was not the silence of absence,
Or of death, but of presence and of speech: life.
My tears and I were embraced by this presence,
By its infinite gentleness: my heart was singing,
My mind was thinking, and my soul was rejoicing.
My hand found its way to his bottle of wine.
Our glasses were filled— with the nectar of life.
Our eyes met: human presence has spoken.

My mind was pregnant, ready for labor--
For hope, for courage, for understanding,
When the tavern bell sounded its call for closure.
As if the flow of time stops—here or there!
As if the time of joy stops—now or then!
Alas! The time of people stops, and it stopped then.
The time of people is a prison—a prison of death.
A toast of joy was exchanged between us.
The stranger stretched his arms, not to salute me,
Not to thank me, not even to bid me good-bye,
But to embrace me! In this embrace, I melted,
Fused in the abyss of his radiance: gentleness.
"Until we meet again....Until we meet again!"

Part II

"Again?" I shouted in the stillness of the night,
Night of my soul, alone with his gentleness!
The ground under my feet was singing,
The moon above my head was smiling,
And the breeze around me was crooning
As I walked in the alleys of my town,
Alone, but not lonely, in the abyss of that again!
Can there be adventures, surprises, or prowling,
Secrets, hiding places, or promises
In the abyss of that embrace?
My heart leaped out of my chest for that again!

My mind was swept with a storm of curiosity,
My heart with impatience, and my will with desire
To feel the magical warmth of that wine drinker.
Oh, how I craved a sip of his rare wine!
Oh, how I craved a peek into his soul,
Into the last moment of his trial on the cross!
And so I became an inhabitant of the night
A wanderer of the desolate alleys of my town
In search of the wine drinker—find of my life.
Many a day and many a night passed fruitlessly
Until one evening, amid a violent storm,
When the sky was thundering and the earth quaking,
My weary legs sought shelter in a tavern—
Yes, a tavern on the northern edge of my town.

On the edge—always on the edge!
"Do we always live on the edge--" I wondered,

"The edge of an experience, of a period, of a place?
Are we always caught in the process of flow—
 Always in transition from one edge to another?"
Well, the tavern was crowded with drinkers:
People drinking and talking in dim light and loud music.
My immediate impulse aimed at a quiet corner
Where I could enjoy a glass of wine peacefully,
Away from the noise of the storm, and the crowd.
I was looking for such a corner when suddenly
I found myself in the net of two inquiring eyes,
Eyeing me, as if I was apprehended in a criminal act.

I am a prowler, after all, and I am a thief,
Not a thief of money or gold, you know,
But of precious treasures of the human soul:
What makes it laugh, live, and die.
Call it guilt, if you please, but I froze in place,
Aground between the storm and those two eyes.
I stared at them timidly, seeking a safe haven,
But they were friendly eyes, and they sparkled,
Not with curiosity but with rapt interest,
As if to say, "Oh, it is you! He is waiting for you!"
"But, alas! The One is always waiting for us!"
A tremor reverberated in my mind and in my heart
"Who is he? A messenger? A wine drinker?" I reflected.

The head that carried those two friendly eyes
Gently nodded with an air of confidence
 And then wafted a furtive look to his right side,
Toward the eastern side of the tavern.
Mystery of mysteries! Does the human soul

Need training, guidelines, or introductions
To consult its desires, fears, or reason,
To feel at home with a kindred soul—
To see its truth, to uphold it, to converse with it?
I felt the luminous presence of this bartender.
I understood him, and he understood me.
A surge of peace filled my anxious heart
And a grateful smile danced in my eyes!

As I left the tumult of the festive crowd behind
And moved closer to the solitary, dim corner,
A ray of light beamed from its very core.
It was not an ordinary kind of light;
It was a magical, mesmerizing beam of light
That carries you by its grace to its source.
And to that source I gravitated, unconsciously,
Yet with the fullness of my knowledge and desire.
There he was sitting in the same posture
Solemnly gazing into the infinite depth of the dark,
Next to his bottle of wine with two empty glasses,
As if he was ready to share a toast with someone.
Before that lonely gaze I stood, transfixed—

But not my heart and indeed not my mind!
I was relishing the warmth of his presence,
Its radiance, awe-inspiring and uplifting,
When he slowly withdrew his solemn gaze
From that infinite depth, away from that Holy place,
And steered it toward my eager gaze.
Alas! His gaze was transformed into a smile,
The same compassionate, welcoming smile

I received as a gift in our first encounter.
Oh, how wonderful it is to be so welcomed!
I watched him fill our glasses with his wine.
Could I speak, and could I understand,
Without a drink of his wine—nectar of The One?

"To your health!" He toasted with a compassionate smile.
Oh, my dear, I floated on this smile as a swallow
Floats dreamily in the sky of a spring day
Held tight in the warmth of his compassion.
But my anxious soul was restless—impatient,
And with fear in my throbbing heart, I confessed:
"My mind has been aching from a brutal thirst,
From an insistent desire to sate some nagging questions
About your last encounter with the primate.
In posing them to you, I seek enlightenment."
The same compassionate smile lingered on his lips,
The same warmth tarried around my soul,
And the same cheerful complexion adorned his face!

"The volcano of agony inflicted on your body
And the wicked torture on your soul and mind
Were undoubtedly crushing and an unbearable hell—
How could a famished person, famished to death,
Endure this hell, defy death, and survive it?
What ordinary person could have endured this hell?"
His smile never left his lips as I was talking.
And with the same smile hovering around his eyes
He helped himself to a sip of wine and then said:
"Every human being can endure the hell of the primate,
And every human being can also defy the death of men."

Suddenly he stopped as if he was lost in deep thought.
Bold furrows stretched over his broad forehead.

"Do you mean in virtue of a soul in them?"
"Not at all!" he promptly countered.
"The idea of soul is a farce, an invention, a fiction
Created by certain men in their own image to one end:
To control their fellow human beings, to subjugate them.
This idea is a most effective means of oppression.
They do it in the name of compassion and reformation!
This idea is the fiercest enemy of joy and peace."
"And yet I have been a prowler," I thought to myself,
"A thief of the most precious treasures of the soul!"
Squeezed by the challenge of my life, I asked:
"You speak in riddles, friend; your language is hard.
Can you explain your words in simpler language?"

"Have you ever conceived the actuality of soul?
Can you? Can anyone? Tell me!" he started.
"Those in power, the august body of the church,
Want you to believe that soul is a unique reality,
Imperceptible, indestructible, self-same, whole,
That it is the seat of reason and the emotions,
Thus, it is the ultimate basis of human life and destiny,
And that God, in His infinite magnificence and beneficence,
Created soul from his own essence for man's happiness,
Therefore, people are dearest to his heart: a prize creation.
They also claim that God gave priests the keys to human destiny:
Knowledge of the divine will, and how to apply it.

"For them, people are creatures, not autonomous beings:

Their life does not depend on their will, or on their reason.
And yet, they foist on us the idea that people,
The true children of God, the jewel of his heart,
Are free and responsible agents--like their father.
Have you heard of a more ridiculous travesty?
What would the idea of heaven and hell,
Eternal bliss and damnation, be without belief in soul?
You see, the very idea of God and cosmic creation
Is a delicious fantasy created by the priest,
As a means of control, at first as an instrument
Of imposing order and the conditions of culture,
But later on as an instrument of power: glory.

"Can the priest's idea of God The Father
Be thought without the concept of soul? Think with me!
The idea of God is used to establish the idea of soul
And the idea of soul to establish the idea of God.
But the sinister aspect of this weird logic is the claim
That the soul, the image of the Father, the Creator,
Is an inert soul: deathless and changeless--lifeless.
Please, tell me: how can an inert, lifeless entity
Be responsible for life—thinking, feeling, and willing?
How can it give rise to the activity of life?
And how can it reflect God's creative essence?
I beg you, friend, not to listen to those imposters,
At least not hastily, but instead to your inner voice!

"Delve into that depth, into that mystery,
Not the mystery of the mountain, or the sun,
No, but the mystery that gives rise to them!
Probe into that world in the night of your soul—

Be patient! Be alert! Be true to what you see!
Do you see an entity you can call soul?
Alas! Do you see any borders, gates, or windows?
Do you see any limits to the mountains, seas, and plains?
Do you see the landscape of this amazing world?
But you see! How do you see? By what power?
By what light do you see what you see?
Now follow the rays that illumine your vision
From one end to the other—to their source!

"Stand before that dazzling sight for a moment.
Penetrate with your eyes the glitter of the glow.
Do not worry! You will not be blinded!
How far does your vision go? Is there a limit?
Can you comprehend what you see? Of course not!"
And with a tremulous smile in his eyes, he cried:
"You are this glow! Yes, you are this shining spark!"
And my body, my mind?" I could not help but ask.
His smile stalked out of his eyes to his lips:
"Yes, do you need me to tell you what you, alone,
Can see when you undertake this inner venture?
The truth of your being shines as a sun inside you.
It is wiser to seek it in that wondrous garden!

"But as for me," he continued thoughtfully,
"My body and every real element of my being
Are emanations from that depth--that spark:
They are a living testimony to the glory of The Light!
You and I are gifts of this light, children of life.
Light is our source, and light is our destiny."
"What about the rest of humankind," I broke in.

"Ah, my brothers and sisters," he exclaimed,
"They too are sparks of light, children of The Light."
"And then? What went wrong?" I am puzzled.
They seem to live in the dark—so do I!" I admitted.
His chest was heaving as if he was running at full speed.
Then, focusing his tender eyes on mine, he whispered:

"I did too!" He abruptly vanished into a cloud of silence,
Pensive silence, creating a moment of sizzling suspense.
His look froze on his face, and his face froze in the silence.
He must have been in a deep struggle with inner forces.
But then, slowly, he regained possession of my attention:
"And then? Why? I understand you!" he said sympathetically.
"I cannot answer or explain your query, though fair,
But I can say to you that the primate was right:
I am a renegade, a runaway from the justice of men,
From their ways, but not from my brothers and sisters.
For them, I live, and for them, I am willing to die.
But my way is different from the ways of men."
He raised his head a little, and then fixed his eyes on me:

"You see," he continued with a melancholy voice.
"The primate was a renegade, a rebel like me!"
A wave of amazement settled on my face.
"A traitor!" My puzzled mind shouted inside me.
He saw the puzzlement on my face, and he read it.
He reads the language of the heart too!
"Not really!" he interrupted my impulsive train of thought.
"We were collaborators in the quest for The Light.
One day his vision blackened and his will was broken
Under the brutal pressure of the supreme council.

He is a good man, according to the justice of men,
And a good man still, one who can live
From the inner spark, if only—" he suddenly stopped.

Lost in deep thought, he involuntarily stretched
His hand to the bottle of wine and softly,
Unaware of what his hands were doing or how,
Poured wine in my glass and then in his,
Trying to quench a thirsty throat, perhaps his soul,
And with the same melancholy eyes, he continued:
"Yes, if only we can find our way to The Light,
If only we can remove the veil from the eyes of men,
If only we can turn their attention inward,
To the light of the spark: our true being."
"The veil? What do you mean, friend?" I asked.
"The veil that dims the light of the mind—its sight:
False belief and bad habits of the mind.

"How can we think, feel," he exclaimed,
"Yes, and how can we will without the spark,
Or how can we see who or what we are,
Or how can we find our way in our quest for The One?"
"What you say is to the point," I said,
"May I ask you to comment on a question?"
"Of course, you may! Conversing with you is a delight!"
"When your body was being devoured by the hell
The primate created for you on the cross,
When this hell was spouting balls of agony
Into your body and anguish into your soul,
When clouds of doubt moved into your mind
You were almost on the verge of giving up—

"Of surrendering your soul and body to the primate;
But you did not—what happened then, tell me, please!"
The glitter in his eyes almost lit our dim booth!
"At that crucial moment, when the flames of hell
Were consuming my frail body bit by bit,
An exquisite feeling crept into my languid soul,
The likes of which I had never felt or known.
It came from the depth, that inscrutable Depth.
It was not of pain that makes your body squeak,
Not of hope that makes your soul wait,
And not of desire that makes your mind anxious—
It was the brightest flash of consciousness ever!
I felt I was on the edge—the edge of Being!

"One foot was tethered on the side of being
And the other on the side on not-being,
Slowly slipping into the arms of not-being.
Alas! My groin was stretching and screeching:
The earth under my other foot was quaking--
Yes, all within the flames of my burning hell.
 Oh, no, the hell the primate created for me
Was not the real hell—not for me, not at all!
My real hell loomed in that flash of consciousness,
On that edge—in the jaws of being and not-being:
Here on this edge lies real hell: the hell of annihilation—
Being slowly crushed by its ferocious teeth,
Being ruthlessly masticated by its fearless jaws!

"Hell is the agony that oozes from these jaws,
And this very agony opened the eyes of my mind
To the ultimate question of my life: being or not-being!

How can you wonder about this question, tell me,
And how can you grasp its meaning or value
If you do not plunge into its ruthless jaws—
If you do not confront its abyss, not-being,
If you do not drink a cup of this abyss?
I was enveloped by that flash of consciousness,
By its luminous radiance, its magical warmth,
When I suddenly heard a voice from the depth:
Remain true to yourself! Be the self you are!

"On the horizon of that blessed consciousness
An opaque image of the primate hovered
With the same gaze and the same frigid face.
To my surprise, from the corner of my battered ear
I heard the same voice and the same temptation:
You still have time; you can receive your glory
If you desist from your quest for The One.
Alas! I and my quest are two in one,
one in two, light in being, and being in light.
This revelation shone in my languid consciousness
Like a morning sun on a beautiful spring day:
Being I seek, and a seeker of The Light I have been,
Light I seek, and a seeker of The One I have been.

"A flash of light illuminated my troubled mind:
I saw the horns of my dilemma fair and square--
Put all the gold of the world, and all its glory,
In one scale and the soul of a human being,
Yes, her life and dignity in the other; if you do,
The scale of gold and glory will tumble down
And will tatter into the hell of people,

Into that permanent pit of fire: extinction.
Yes, the way of the primate is the way of extinction,
Not the way of being, and not the way of life.
But life is growth—growth from The Light
And in the light, not from gold, and not in glory.
I am a seeker of The Light, a lover of The Sun.

"A ray of this sun danced before my eyes.
At that moment, I was one with this ray,
At ease with myself—an exuberant drop of life!
Life is a surge—an unstoppable flood of being.
The more I felt the intensity of this surge
The stronger, the clearer, and the more hopeful I became.
Hope is the ultimate fountain of faith: submission,
Not retreat, not submission to fear, to cowardice,
To ignorance, or to weakness, but to understanding,
The kind that surpasses human understanding: love!
Yes, I had to choose between two ways,
The way of people or the way of The Light.
I chose the way of light: the way of love.

Part III

"The air of love is the only air worth breathing.
Not only my lungs but also my entire being,
Was pulsating with a warm breeze of this air
As the flames of hell were ravaging my body.
You know," he began to speak softly and slowly,
"I have always felt from the core of my heart,
That love is the beginning and the end;
It is the primal source, yes, the very source,

Of being: life in all its forms, in all its colors.
Love is the spirit that animates life itself,
The mind of this magnificent world and its heart.
It is the source of beauty and its splendor.
Beauty is consecrated by the hands of love!

Be a tree of love: give your fruits freely.
Love is a sumptuous banquet: invite your friends.
Be a renegade, a follower of The Light,
Not a prowler, not a thief of human treasures.
You are the real treasure: seek yourself.
Seeking is the life of love—of giving absolutely.
The more you give, the more you can give,
The more you will be: being is supremely good!
Does the good need to justify its supremacy,
The jewel its brilliance, and the sun its light?
Be a stream of being, flowing from the heart.
Pour yourself in the infinite ocean of being
And return to the world as a beam of light!"

His eyes were firing arrows of exhilaration.
Drops of sweat were shining on his forehead
When he gently, and with passion in his eyes,
Fixed a pregnant gaze at his wine glass
As if to reveal a feeling of thirst for some wine.
I was swept by the candor of his gaze
And regained my consciousness when he lost his.
Like bees in a rose bed, a throng of questions
Were buzzing in my mind, crying for answers.
Like bees in a rose bed for urgent answers.
Foremost among those questions was a desire

To inquire about the experience this renegade had,
To know what he truly felt and thought on the cross,
And what led him to those insights about love.

He was still swimming in the sea of that gaze
When I filled his glass with his nectar.
"And you?" he exclaimed as if taken by surprise.
The time was ripe to move closer to him,
Although he was closer to me than the blood in my veins:
"You have piqued my curiosity," I began,
And with a heavy heart and a bashful look, I asked:
"I am interested in the last moments on the cross
When the eyes of the primate abandoned your sight—
What exactly happened during those moments?"
"Those moments were an indescribable adventure!"
Then the air of our booth froze into silence.

The silence the human soul yearns for
Is more articulate, and certainly more elegant,
Than the silence in the absence of the heart--of love.
The soul feels the fire of love in human silence.
 "The Truth is silence?" He said very softly.
Alas! Was he drowned in its infinite ocean?
In the belly of infinity, you do not feel or see.
How can you feel or see if you are so drowned?
And yet, I was possessed by a forceful urge
To know the secret of his venture on the cross.
My blood was throbbing fast and hard in my temples.
It was a moment of confusion! A moment of embarrassment!
A moment of frustration! A moment of hope!

Do you know, dear, that the human soul,
The loving soul, whose love lives from The Truth,
In The Truth, in the bosom of primal innocence,
Is indifferent to the silly ambitions of human beings?
The soul of that gentle renegade saw what I felt
And felt the perplexity of my mind--he understood.
He spoke without speaking and gave without giving.
Does the sun give light because it wants to or cares?
His face glowed with compassion--he was his face.
Its rays flowed into my heart: I became a pulse of life.
The storm of perplexity that was raging there,
Wreaking havoc in the world of my feeble mind,
Suddenly knelt obediently at their feet: peace!

His glowing face was still the sun of the moment
When the ashes of my perplexity were resurrected
Into a lucid feeling of courage: I was whole again.
"What exactly happened," I asked involuntarily,
"When the flames of hell were ravaging your body
And the pangs of agony were rocking your consciousness,
When the ruthless eyes of death were mocking you?
Did you feel their sarcasm? Were you ready to die?
Did you feel their sweet revenge, their feeling of triumph?
You drew for me a vivid picture of the hell
The primate created for you, and you alone,
And you spoke of your body as if it were a possession,
An instrument, and yet you were suffering its agony!

"The fire of hell was yours, the agony was yours,
And the eyes of death were fastened on your wasting body—
Did you die on the cross, as many people now think?

Alas! You are here, but are you here?
Something about those moments eludes my mind."
The train of my questions came to a halt
When his complexion suddenly wore a garb of serenity.
His eyes, to which mine were a willing captive,
Now scrutinized me with profound empathy.
Their arms embraced me, warmly and tightly.
I felt as though I was on the wings of a lark
Soaring freely and joyfully into the dome of heaven.
Those eyes spoke the language of human presence.

Human presence is the soil in which love grows and ripens.
It is the garden, in which two human beings connect,
Celebrate the rite of freedom from convention,
Feel the synchronized rhythm of their pulsating hearts,
And dance to this rhythm the dance of their lives.
Here their lives flow from their hearts
As the river flows from its spring--spontaneously.
In that solitary corner, in that dim booth,
I felt the radiance of human presence: His presence.
I felt the impact of its sublime mystery.
I have been a prowler, yes, and a thief
Only because I had been homeless, rootless.
Here in that radiance, I felt at home, rooted.

"The star of love," he said with a flare of kindness,
With eyes staring into the void of our dim booth,
"Has always been the fountain of inspiration, of light—
Of the courage to think, to feel, and to will:
I am, and I thrive, in virtue of this light.
If it were to be eclipsed, or fade away,

I shall slowly shrink and then fade away.
The world of ordinary people is hostile to this star:
Do you know they take a long nap when it appears?
Light blinds their eyes and stultifies their hearts.
When their police discover someone awake,
Taking a peek at its radiance during their slumber
They immediately apprehend him and then try him!

"Then mercifully they give him a reformation sentence.
If a person repeats the same capital offense
He will be placed in a permanently dark room.
But if someone discovers the light of this star
If he relishes the beauty of this star—its truth,
If he is convinced of its worth and power,
And seeks to explore the depth of its mysteries,
He has one choice: to defect and be a renegade.
This is a momentous decision: to choose what you are!
And you are the only treasure you have in this life!
This is the only reality you can love—love in The One.
Everything else, social or natural, is external to you:
They are temporary puffs in the passing show of nature!

"I chose to be a renegade, a fighter of darkness,
A seeker of that distant yet near Star-- of its light,
Of its rays of wisdom, of its power of love!
You see, when you live by the wisdom of these rays,
When they become the moving spirit of your action,
You become one with them: they shine through you.
They illumine the sky of your mind, and of your heart;
They infuse your heart with the passion of life: love.
Then you cannot hide; you become a lightning bug!

But the primate is an intelligent and knowing man.
He knows the ways of the stars, and the ways of men.
He established a special force to catch these bugs:
Stargazers are insolent intruders—disturbers of the peace!

"But the star I now seek is only a guardian angel,
A messenger from The One: a star of all lightning bugs!
I am not versed in the ways of lightning bugs,
And I cannot live in darkness, not for long.
One afternoon, during the usual nap, I made a stir,
I hovered over the sleeping flock and fluttered a little.
A few eyes were open and were staring at me!
Wide open, they chased me everywhere I moved,
But the intelligent eyes of the primate were there
Waiting for me at every corner and at every door,
Watchful of my moves and ready for a prized prey!
I did not resist those eyes or their advances,
But froze in place and then in their hands.
A sturdy dark cage was my prison for many a day.
Light was forbidden—a contaminant, a harmful agent.

"In nailing me to the cross the way he did,
In trying to roast my body with the heat of this hell,
He really was aiming at my soul, not at my body;
He was aiming at the light that lit my inner sanctuary:
The source of my being, the reason for my being.
He knew he could not extinguish its light or dim it--
How could anyone destroy the indestructible?
No, he aimed to test my will, my resolve,
To seek The One, to get closer to The Light.
The primate is a shrewd gambler, a ruthless ruler,

Protective of his flock and devoted to his own glory.
He knew I would accept his hell, and withstand it,
But whether I could stand it—that was the rub.

"The cross was my baptismal basin, made especially for me,
The fire was my holy water, the primate was the archpriest!
He wanted to baptize me with his two holy hands
And fashion me in his image as a member of his flock!
His ultimate aim was to keep me out, a thorn in his side;
He needed a convert—a zealot, a fighter of The Light.
He needed a policeman, not a lawyer, and not a judge—
How else could he keep his kingdom safe from the light?
You see, he tried his usual method of seduction,
Of giving me all the wealth and all the power, yes,
And all the glory my heart could desire, or hope for,
And I am convinced he would have stood by his word,
Not to protect my wellbeing, but his own kingdom.

But that was not the end of his patience, not yet--
"Not of his endeavor to bend or subjugate my will,
To to dim the light of the spark, of love, in my heart,
To make me a convert to the ways of people.
The cross was the last station for me, and for him;
It was the borderline—the test of my will, and his.
The point of the hell he invented for me, of its agony,
Was first to give me a glimpse of death,
Of the non-existence of my body, of my life.
He wanted me to see with my whole being
The magnitude of my impending loss, of all my work!
He sought to distill my life into a nutshell, to see it,
To put it in the palm of my hand and evaluate it.

"I did! Do you know that during that moment,
As my body was crackling in the flames of pain
Something glorious, something magical, happened to me?
A smile surged from the depth of my heart, warm and bold,
Onto my tremulous lips: they were dry and thirsty.
It climbed upward to my droopy eyes where my soul resides,
 Where the flames of agony were raging on all sides,
And from there shone as a bright star of love.
The loveless eyes of the primate saw its bright light
And fixed a stare at me: love is his worst enemy,
The enemy he could not tame or defeat, or seduce.
 His eyes, cold and still, darted vibes of fury my way:
He felt my smile. He understood. He vanished.

"Just before this last conversation with the primate,"
Unable anymore to control my inquisitive mind,
For my mind reached a pivotal peak of suspense, I broke in:
"What exactly happened, not only what you felt?
During that decisive moment of inner transformation?"
The serenity, dear reader, with which he began his account
Was suddenly transfigured into a vivid image of solemnity,
An awe-inspiring expression, neither frightful nor simple.
Shivers of hesitation, perhaps wonder, streamed into my heart
And, like flashes of thunder, crashed into my temples!
Slowly, and with an effort coming from the depth—
 Of his eyes--He grasped my puzzled face with a sad gaze.
My bewildered gaze sank deeper into puzzlement, into suspense.

Oh, how I wish I remained a captive to that gaze!
How I wish I remained a captive to its warmth!
Does it matter whether it was sad, happy, or hopeful

As long as you are in the lap of human presence?
As long as you are upheld by its light: love?
My rumination was interrupted by the sudden appearance
Of the bartender with a new bottle of his wine.
Respectfully he filled our empty bottles.
Why did he show up at that very moment?
Did he feel the effulgence of His presence?
The human heart feels in mysterious ways.
The bartender disappeared the way he had appeared,
Imperceptibly, gently, like a waft of a spring breeze.

But that solemn gaze did not linger on his face:
The air of solemnity was gradually transformed
Into a glow of humility: home of authenticity.
Rays of tenderness flowed from under his eyebrows.
 He must have been in the throes of torment.
Frankly, dear reader, I was not an indifferent spectator.
Before a spectacle of this amazing transformation
I was a participant, and, please, do not ask why!
How could I remain indifferent in the absence
Of a barrier that separated me from his shining soul?
I was enveloped by his presence, by two arms of love.
I was one with it, yes, and in it: I was charmed.
A soft smile gleamed from this glorious presence:

"Describing the inner life of the human heart,
Its innermost being, thrusting for that core,
Is a supremely daunting, and almost forbidding task.
We meet a forward enemy on the way: vanity.
This is an enemy of entrapment, of sly deception.
With a seductive wink, it tries to lure your eyes

Into yourself, magnifying the size of your vision
So you perceive the size of your real self infinitely bigger than it is,
More beautiful, more significant, wiser than it is.
 You cling to yourself and away from its real truth.
Conceit always lurks on the border of consciousness.
I am weary of this enemy; I am tired of its snares.

"But then, what if I stand on that mountaintop
Of my inner being, seek to grasp it with my vision?
What if I delve deeper into its inner fountain,
Into that primal fountain, into that eternal sun,
Whose magnificent brilliance blinds our eyes?
How can I, this simple ray, this minuscule part,
Comprehend the truth, the splendor of this brilliance,
Of this infinite whole?" He stopped for a moment
And then, beaming with the same thoughtfulness,
Continued: "When you are within that brilliance
You do not think, you do not feel, and you do not will:
How can you be aware of your mind and body?
You become a pure, infinite existence; you become one with The
Sun.

"You become a drop of light; you become a drop of love: silence!
"Try to remember what your eyes saw, or your mind thought,
Or your heart felt when you returned from this venture.
Being resists the advances of thought; it mocks it.
Thought, splendid and resourceful in its ways,
Stands as a ridiculous presence before the eyes of being,
And memory, this strong pillar of thought and practice,
Has neither a hand nor a back on which to carry
The life of being: what is an abstraction to life?

What is appearance, or show, to infinite reality?
What you bring with you from that marvelous venture
Are not ideas, or feelings, or images, or even messages?
What you bring is a new self: a drop of love!

"Just before my conversation with the primate,
When I extended to him a smile from my heart
And his ruthless eyes became stiff like a rock—
Yes, when I was able to take hold of myself,
Of my fears and desires: when I became indifferent
To the pain of my body and the glory of the world,
When I stood totally naked before my own eyes
Free from attachment to everything that was I,
In the presence of that glowing spark within,
Yes, when I stood naked before that spark, my real self,
Yes, even when the flames of agony were eating my flesh,
I made my decision to renounce the world, and my body,
And cleave to the spark that glowed in my heart!

"I became one with it; I was its glow--its pure glow.
The spark that was in my heart became my heart
And I became my heart. A miracle happened then-
The flames of pain that were eating my flesh,
The agony of my soul that was ravishing my will,
And the doubt that was clouding the vision of my mind,
Vanished! Everything around me and in me—
Yes, my body, the eyes of the primate, and the cross,
All vanished: I was neither here nor there,
Neither this nor that, neither happy nor sad;
I was a warm pulse of life—a drop of love.
Love does not speak; it is speech: human silence.
I was that drop of speech on the cross: I was that smile!

"I was in The One, and The One was in me: I was The One
In its infinite plentitude, performing the rite of being.
I was not a stretch of consciousness—an observer,
And I was not a self-consciousness—a subject, a seeker.
The seeker in me became the sought: love.
The more I worshipped at its luminous altar,
The more I cuddled in its gentle arms, its warmth,
The clearer I heard its call: I yearn for you!
Oh, how I yearn for the arms of The One!
I sat in its lap and leaned against its chest.
Its heartbeats were music to my ears: enchanted.
They were singing the hymn of eternal creation.

"Warm tears rolled on my cheeks and onto my lips.
I felt their power, and I felt their warmth.
They did not come from my eyes; they came from His.
 I enjoyed their aroma, and I relished their taste.
They were nectar to my palate: tears of love.
Then I looked up into His brilliant eyes,
Into their infinite depth, into their magical fountain.
Deeper I looked, and deeper I delved, unchecked:
The beginning is the end, and the end is the beginning,
An infinite river of being, a burst of eternal creation.
Worlds of being stretched on both sides of this river—
Of beauty, of truth, and of life, all in a joyful dance.
They were rays of light, one in the radiant One.

When I returned from the glorious visit in His lap
I began to see with new eyes and feel with a new heart.
Now I see with His eyes and feel with His heart.
Now I see all in The One, and I see The One in all.

I do not see things and worlds hanging in nothing.
One starry night I took a walk in the Garden,
Where every kind of flower grows, and every beauty thrives.
On the way, I stopped at the foot of the mountain and asked it:
"Where do you stand? What makes you strive upward?"
With a puzzled face and a puzzled voice, it said:
"Ask The One; He knows!" Then I went to the moon
And to every flower of The Garden with the same question.
All in one tongue said: "Ask the One; He knows!"

"You see, I am a seeker of The Light, and yes,
I am a renegade to the eyes of the primate.
But I am a lover! My world is not the world of people.
It is the world of The Sun: I live from within,
Not from without, from the fire of the spark.
The cross was the limit; it was the edge.
There my heart was filled with the light of love.
No, I did not seek eternal life on the cross.
There was no room in my heart for desire—
Not for wisdom or glory, and not for being his Son.
The only cry I heard was the cry of love, for more love.
The only nectar I sought was the nectar of love.
A ray of light is a ray of yearning for The One.

"I am not the Son of God, as some people say;
I became a human being, a ray of light, on the cross.
There, the hand of The One touched my hand: union.
This is the mystery of the cross; this is the glory of love."
At that very point of his gripping account,
And without knowing how, I simply interrupted
That lover, that prince of revolt, that shining star,

With a desire to inquire about his present identity,
But he suddenly vanished from my sight.
I looked around in the dark with bewildered eyes.
Instead of the renegade, I saw the bartender.
He filled my glass from His bottle of wine.
I drank it: a star glittered in my mind.

www.ingramcontent.com/pod-product-compliance
Lightning Source LLC
Chambersburg PA
CBHW071838090426
42737CB00012B/2287